D0405571

PRAYERS FROM THE HEART

Honor Books
Tulsa, Oklahoma

Prayers from the Heart
ISBN 1-56292-636-5

P.O. Box 55388
Tulsa, OK 74155

Printed in China.

Introduction

Bound within the pages of this book are the extraordinary prayers of ordinary people from all walks of life. People like you and me. People who walk daily with God on the mountaintops as well as in the valleys of life. As you read these simple prayers, it is our hope that the heart of your own prayer life will be enhanced and you will move into a deeper, richer personal relationship with God.

In order to ensure that these prayers contain something special for every reader, we have chosen three verses from each book of the Bible and asked our writers to reflect on one Scripture in particular while penning their prayers. The result is a rich tapestry of human experience woven into a broad base of biblical perspective—God's words to man, coupled with man's words to God. We hope that this will help you better understand not only the human condition but also the character and intentions of God as He reaches out His hand of love to you.

It is our prayer that no matter who you are, whether man or woman, young or old, lifelong Christian or earnest seeker of truth, you will find strength and encouragement in these prayers from the heart. And as you move through these pages, you will be able to peer beyond the superficial and into the depths of God's love and grace.

God bless you as you read.

Honor Books would like to thank the following individuals
who graciously shared prayers from their hearts
in order to make this book possible:

Rev. David Alldredge
Nanette Anderson
Editha Ann Bammesberger
Freda Ann Brink
Rebecca Currington
Sherry Doherty
Susan Downs
Rick Edwards
Amy Gilroy
Debbie Salter Goodwin
JoNell Hafer
Elece Hollis
Christina M. Honea
Sarah M. Hupp
Cleo Justus
Tommy Justus
Everett Leadingham
Janie L. McGee
William H. McMurry III
Jim Morgan
Jimmy D. Peacock
Shawna Rickard
Peggy Rooney
Rhonda Scocos
Debra White Smith
Jeff Thomas

God created man in his own image, in the image of God he created him; male and female he created them.
GENESIS 1:27

Dear Father,

I close my eyes and remember the many wonders of Your creation. My mind is awash with images: butterflies gliding along on unseen currents, brilliant flames of light kissing the morning sky, countless shades of green playing outside in my yard. I see the earth preparing for its winter sleep and coaxing itself awake with the sights, sounds, and smells of spring. You have created a world that entertains us with kaleidoscopes of brilliance.

As my eyes take in the wonder of Your creative power, I find it difficult to consider my own creation. You created me not in the form of the brilliant sun, the majestic eagle, or the mighty mountain, but as a man made of nothing more than dust filled with Your breath, oh God.

I praise You because in all Your infinite wisdom, You chose to mold me in Your image—the created walking in the very image of the Creator. It is as though creation is Your mural, and I am Your signature. As a child who honors his proud heritage and carries on the memories of his father, so I am proud of the responsibility and family name I have been given by You. Thank You for loving me so much that even angels recognize me as a child of God.

Amen.

Who made a person's mouth? And who makes someone deaf or not able to speak?
Or who gives a person sight or blindness?
It is I, the LORD.
EXODUS 4:11 NCV

Ah, Lord God!

How many times I forget that You are in control. I become so absorbed in my own struggles, my own joys, my own projects, my own schedule, that when another commitment or problem crosses my path, I only wonder how "I" am going to handle it.

When I turn my eyes inward, Lord, I lose sight of Your power, Your greatness, Your sovereignty, Your timing in every situation. I forget that those things I perceive as struggles are the very things that will make me grow. When I focus on my abilities, I come away feeling inadequate. When I focus on Your abilities, I come away feeling strong. Only in Your strength can I truly understand another person's needs, sense someone else's hurt, love another by listening. Help me to bear in mind that when I turn my heart to my own selfishness, I am of no use to anyone, not even myself.

Forgive me, Lord, for forgetting that You are in charge. Keep me focused on You today, more than on myself. Thank You for giving me Your wisdom to guide me and Your strength to help me follow Your way. Help me to be a blessing to others and pleasing in Your eyes.

Amen.

Be holy, for I, the LORD your God, am holy.
LEVITICUS 19:2 NAB

Loving God,

In the course of my life, the question of holiness has arisen often. What does it mean to be holy? Where do I go to learn holiness?

In my formative years, I knew only the teachings of my elders, who taught me that Your Ten Commandments are non-negotiable and that You are a stern God Whose precepts are uncompromising. As I grew older, I decided that holiness meant giving, so I gave from my abundance to those less fortunate. *Surely my good deeds will be pleasing to You and I will be reckoned holy in Your sight*, I reasoned. But I soon realized that I was simply dividing my worldly goods into categories, measuring my holiness in terms of my finances.

Then, loving God, in Your mercy You took pity on my immature and self-righteous ways. You shared with me Your wisdom. I came to understand that to be holy is to imitate You, not in Your greatness but in Your humbleness. You have called me to give as You have given to me—quietly and selflessly. I can do this only when my good deeds are performed out of a pure love for You and for humankind. Please help me to always lead a holy life by continually walking in Your love and humility.

Amen.

The LORD *bless thee, and keep thee: The* LORD *make his face shine upon thee, and be gracious unto thee: The* LORD *lift up his countenance upon thee, and give thee peace.*
NUMBERS 6:24-26 KJV

My Father,

I know You gave this blessing to Moses and Aaron and they were to pronounce it over the people of Israel. But when I read it, I want to claim it for myself! I want to be so close to You that Your face is always shining on me. I want Your countenance, that holy expression of Your thoughts and feelings, to be lifted up before me as well—that I might grasp Your loving affection toward me; that I might learn Your ways and know those things that please You and displease You; that I might find peace and security for my life.

Lord, I long for peace that will allow me to rest calmly and securely in a world full of conflict. I want the kind of peace that lasts forever and does not rise and fall according to my circumstances.

Please, oh heavenly Father, bless me also with the blessing You pronounced over Moses and Aaron. Let Your face shine on me with the love of a father for his child. Be gracious to me, Your child, for I have no strength in myself. And lift up Your countenance upon me and give me peace.

Amen.

And thou shalt love the LORD *thy God with all thine heart, and with all thy soul, and with all thy might.*
DEUTERONOMY 6:5 KJV

Dear God,

How completely worthy of my love You are! Your mercy and grace, Your unconditional love, have rescued me from the ravages of sin. You have never stopped loving me: picking me up out of the messes I've made, chastening me, forgiving me, and restoring me to fellowship with You.

I confess, Father, that my ability to love You back is faulty and limited; my heart is fickle, my soul distracted, and my strength wasted on selfish pursuits. Forgive me for the many times I have ascribed higher worth to anyone or anything other than You. Oh how that must break Your heart; and yet You never give up on me.

Your great persistence helps me to face the truth, Lord—I only love You because You loved me first, demonstrating it with a sacrifice too dear for me to fully comprehend. I determine this day not to move from beneath that never-ending, transforming flow literally poured out on me from the cross. I want to be drenched in it, body and soul, day after eternal day, until I have no other response than to shout, "Oh Lord God, thank You. Thank You! I love You, too!"

Amen.

Have I not commanded you? Be strong and courageous. Do not be terrified; do not be discouraged, for the LORD your God will be with you wherever you go.

JOSHUA 1:9

Mighty God,

What great adventure do You have planned for me today? I can't help but wonder where You will take me and what You have planned for me to do.

You have given me a remarkable vision—one that is bigger than I am and more than I could ever hope to accomplish on my own. I know that I must listen closely to Your voice and carefully follow Your instructions. How faithful You are when I am obedient! What often seems to me to be a small and insignificant step has opened doors and opportunities time and time again. I have seen You work miracles that I would never have believed possible, simply because I ventured out of my comfort zone.

Lord, help me to place my hand in Yours and step carefully onto the path You have set before me. I will not give in to discouragement or fear. I promise to take courage in the fact that You are always with me and there is nothing I must face alone. Today I rejoice knowing that there is much that can be done and You have called me to do my part. Help me always to remember that You make all things possible!

Amen.

So may all your enemies perish, O LORD!
But may they who love you be like the sun when
it rises in its strength.
JUDGES 5:31

Heavenly Father,

I love to get up early and experience the beauty of the sun breaking over the horizon to herald a new day. The strength of its fire and light has all of creation reaching upward. Its magnificence seems even more amazing after a season of gray skies and rain. I know that Your love for me is like the sun. It fills my cold heart with strength, with power, and with brilliance.

But there are days, like today, when I feel weak and struggle with doubts. I see the powerful rays of the sun with my eyes, but they cannot seem to break through the clouds in my heart. At other times the pain of loss has been so strong that taking the next breath is difficult, and I shrink back and cloak myself in darkness. Help me, Lord, to let the rays of Your love penetrate the clouds and fill me with sunlight.

Lord, I want the powerful light of Your love to chase away my enemies and open my life to Your undimming truth. I want to radiate the warmth of that light to all those You bring across my path. I want Your love to shine so brightly through me that those who encounter me will be left reaching for its Source.

Amen.

Where you go, I will go. Where you live, I will live.
Your people will be my people, and Your God will be my God.
RUTH 1:16 NCV

Lord,

I wonder if Ruth fully understood the implications of her words to Naomi. Did she really know what it would be like to be a stranger in an unfamiliar land? Did she anticipate how homesick she would feel?

I ask, Lord, because Ruth seems so much braver than I. Here she is, facing so many changes. She had just lost her husband and now she was leaving behind her home, her friends, everything familiar. What courage she must have had. I'm not so good at facing change, Lord. The death of a loved one leaves me with a hole in my heart that never seems to close. A cross-country move leaves me feeling cut off from friends. A change in a career causes me to feel the fearsome stress of learning new ways of doing things and developing new relationships. So, Lord, I need Ruth's courage.

Give me the courage to face change head on, Lord, and the confidence to trust that You will always be there with me no matter what those changes might be. Wipe away my tears of anxiety and replace them with eyes that shine with anticipation. And prepare the way before me, so that "where You go, I will go"—willingly, joyfully, expectantly.

Amen.

Then Eli answered and said, Go in peace: and the God of Israel grant thee
thy petition that thou hast asked of him.
1 Samuel 1:17 KJV

Lord,

I thank You for all the times I have come to You with a petition, just like Hannah, and You spoke the same words to my heart that You spoke to hers, "Go in peace." How faithful You are.

Help me always to remember Your faithfulness. When I come to You with a new petition, bring to my remembrance all those times in the past when You have granted my plea and I have risen up in peace, sad no more. Remembering the past with You, Lord, is a great faith-builder for me. As I recall what You have done, I become reassured that You, my faithful Keeper, will always listen and will always answer and will always "be there" to give me peace.

Lord, I have decided that from now on when I come to You with a petition, I will not get up and go until I can go in peace. If there is doubt, I'll wait and recall Your faithfulness to me until I can go in peace. If there is fear, I will quiet myself by listening to Your Holy Spirit and wait for Your peace to overwhelm me. I will not move until I feel Your peace. But when it comes, I will rise up and go, like Hannah, and be sad no more.

Amen.

The L*ORD* *will do what is good in his sight.*
2 SAMUEL 10:12

Lord,

You can see the big picture and the long-range view. Your vision is perfect and Your perspective is clear. Compared to You, I am blind. I am by all accounts shortsighted, and I focus mostly on what concerns only me. Forgive me for not seeing how You are at work in the world. Give me eyes to see the things that You see: the needs and hurts of others, my own shortcomings and inconsistencies, the beauty and joy of Your creation.

Lord, You are the all-powerful One. You will accomplish what You set out to do. You will not be denied, and what You choose to do will be good. It has to be good, for by definition You are good and all that You do is good. What I want most is to be a part of what You are doing. I want to follow Your plan for me and use the talents and abilities You have given me to further Your work in the world.

Like Joab, David's general, I will prepare wisely and do the best I can with the resources You have given me. Help me to trust in Your vision. Give me strength to follow Your instructions. Thank You for allowing me to be part of Your awesome plan.

Amen.

Observe what the LORD your God requires: Walk in his ways, and keep his decrees and commands, his laws and requirements, as written in the Law of Moses, so that you may prosper in all you do and wherever you go.

1 KINGS 2:3

Lord,

What a wonderful blessing this was—spoken over Solomon by his father, King David. When I read these verses, oh, I wish I could say that to my son. Of course I want him to keep Your charge, to walk in Your ways; to keep Your statutes, Your commandments, Your judgments, and Your testimonies; but not as written in the law of Moses. Please, Lord, guide him according to the "law of love," the new law that Christ brought us.

Oh God, how grateful I am to be able to say to my son, "Everything is in Jesus. Walk in His teachings, live by the principles expressed in His life, embrace His judgments and testimonies." Thank You, Lord, for the New Covenant. Thank You for sending Your only Son to bear our guilt and inadequacy. Thank You for judging us by the "law of love."

I guess what I'm saying, Lord, is thank You for Your grace—the unmerited favor that You pour out upon our lives.

Amen.

Hezekiah trusted in the LORD, the God of Israel. . . .
He held fast to the LORD and did not cease to follow him;
he kept the commands the LORD had given Moses.
And the LORD was with him;
he was successful in whatever he undertook.
2 KINGS 18:5-7

Oh Lord,

Why does it seem that when I try to do good, my good intentions get messed up in misunderstood motives, harsh words, and hard feelings? How can a person like me, with mere human strength, be successful in everything I try to do? It seems impossible, but Your Word says that I can do it if I "hold fast" to You and follow Your commandments.

"Holding fast" is not so easy in today's chaotic world. It seems like every day everything I know changes. I would slip if not for the truth You have revealed to me—that Jesus died for my sins, You resurrected Him from death, and He lives and walks with me today. You are my Savior and the Savior of the world, Jesus. And to that truth, I can "hold fast."

Thank You, Lord, for all You have done for me and for helping me succeed in this world with all its twists and turns. Give me the courage to do my best and trust You to do the rest.

Amen.

Give thanks to the LORD, *call on his name;*
make known among the nations what he has done.
1 CHRONICLES 16:8

Heavenly Father,

I have heard that there is a proper prayer protocol that begins with praise and thanksgiving. Although I am sure there isn't one specific way to come to You, Lord, and talk to You about my life, the gratitude that often washes over me seems an appropriate place to start.

Thank You, God, that You have surrounded me with love. Thank You for both the good and the bad times I have experienced. The bad times have certainly taught me things I probably would not have learned otherwise. The good times make trusting You so much easier. Thank You for the gifts and talents You have blessed me with. Help me acknowledge and use them to honor You. Thank You for sending Your only Son to die in my place, to take my blame. This gift is so undeserved and I am blown away by Your awesome grace. Help me live by faith in the assurance that this grace is mine, Father God.

It feels so good to stop and spend time thanking You for all Your blessings. It feels like putting a long overdue thank-you note in the mailbox. Lord, please receive my humble attempt at thanksgiving—my "thank-you note" prayer.

Amen.

If my people, who are called by my name, will humble themselves and pray and seek my face and turn from their wicked ways, then will I hear from heaven and will forgive their sin and will heal their land.

2 Chronicles 7:14

Merciful God,

Our nation is suffering. Every day there is a new story that depicts the anguish and dysfunction of what we have become. Families are broken and hurting; children are growing up without fathers and mothers that they so desperately need. People are suffering and dying from devastating diseases, and countless numbers are trapped in a life of poverty—alone and without hope. And somehow, defining what is right and true has become blurred in the face of popular opinion.

Lord, forgive me for my indifference. Give me an unshakable burden to pray for this nation. I ask that You awaken hearts and draw them to Yourself. Bless our leaders with wisdom and courage to make righteous decisions that will bring restoration and healing. I thank You for Your endless mercy, for You are the only true solution to the problems that plague our land.

Help me to remember, Lord, that I may never accomplish remarkable things, but I am without excuse if I don't make a difference where You place me. Help me show others that You are the only answer to their seemingly helpless situations.

Amen.

Oh LORD, God of Israel, you are righteous!
EZRA 9:15

My Gracious Father,

I come to You trembling, tears of guilt staining my cheeks once again. I'm not sure exactly what I expect as I approach You, but I know that nothing could be worse than this separation I've felt between us lately. And to think, I chose to be where I am—wandering on my own, rather than enjoying the privilege of being in Your presence.

I guess I thought I could handle life by myself for a while, and by doing so, avoid the guilt that inevitably accompanies my disobedience. But lately I've even been missing that aching inside that warns me that all is not right. I long for the security of Your guidance and, more than anything, the joy of knowing that pleasing You requires only the free and complete surrender of my imperfect love.

So here I am, Father, holding out to You all of my love, the blessings You've entrusted to me, and my imperfections. I lay them at Your feet. But instead of reaching to take them, You hold Your arms open wide and reach for me instead. You welcome me, just as a father welcomes the scolded child who, with teary eyes, holds out arms longing for the hug that assures, "You're accepted, and I love you still."

Amen.

You alone are the L*ORD.*
You made the heavens, even the highest heavens, and all their starry host, the earth and all that is on it, the seas and all that is in them. You give life to everything, and the multitudes of heaven worship you.

NEHEMIAH 9:6

Dear Lord,

I worship You along with the rest of Your creation, knowing that You have created me differently from the rest. You intended me to have an intimacy with You that was impossible for the rest of Your creation. And yet there can be no real intimacy where there is dishonesty and attempts to disguise my true self. Lord, forgive me for thinking that I could hide from You. I don't want You to see my selfishness, neglect, callousness. I want to hide my gossiping, temper tantrums, unkindness, dishonesty, irresponsibility. I want to keep all my human frailties from You—fool You into thinking I'm somebody important, to impress You.

What an absurd creature I am! I'm like the ostrich with his head in the sand, thinking he is safe from view, but in reality, exposing himself in the most unflattering way. Help me to see myself as I truly am.

Help me to be vigilant in my recognition that You are there for every aspect of my life. For it's only in that recognition that I can know Your unfailing love and experience real intimacy with You, my Creator.

Amen.

If you remain silent at this time, relief and deliverance . . .
will arise from another place.
ESTHER 4:14

Lord,

You were gracious to Esther and her people. She was Your chosen person to help deliver her people. Yet You gave her a choice. She could be part of Your plan, or she could choose to step aside and allow Your deliverance to come through someone else.

How merciful You are, Lord God, to give us choices. Esther's choice was a fearsome one. Yet she decided to walk in faith along the path You had laid out for her. And she has been celebrated for centuries because of her courage. Because of her faith. Because she chose You.

Every day I face choices, Lord. I may not be walking into throne rooms, and I may not affect whole nations by my words and actions. But, Lord, I do affect those around me by the choices I make. I do affect others by the way I live my life. Help me to remember Esther. Help me to choose to be part of Your plan, remembering that Your way is always best. Your plan is always right. Your plan will be a blessing for all. Thanks, Lord, for the choices You offer. And thanks for helping me to choose Your will.

Amen.

Again his [God's] *voice roars—*
the majestic sound of his thunder.
He does great things beyond our knowing.
JOB 37:4,5 NAB

Loving God,

As I look out through the beaded raindrops scattered across the windowpane, I see reflected there the glory and the trepidation of Your greatness. The blast of thunder and the glare of lightning being flung to earth from exploding clouds bring both exhilaration and fear. Is this Your way of warning us that You command everything in this world? It is humbling to witness this clash in the sky and to realize how very fragile I am in Your sight.

I wait faithfully for Your mercy, sometimes wondering if You have even heard my cries. But You are the wise One. You are the One Who knows my weaknesses. When I struggle for attention in my supposed grandeur, You teach me modesty. When I believe that my blessings come because of my own virtue, You humble me. When I walk through a storm of my own making, even then, You are with me, sheltering me with Your righteous right hand.

I rejoice in the revelation that You are truly my Father. For only a loving parent would plod unceasingly through the storms of life, carrying the child, until the child is willing to follow. I put my trust in You, Lord. I put my trust in You.

Amen.

Be exalted, O LORD, *in your strength; we will sing and praise your might.*
PSALM 21:13

Oh Father God,

As I focus on You, I exalt You in my mind and heart. You and You alone are my strength. Without You I can do nothing, I am nothing. All that I am is in You. If I am intelligent, it is because You have barely brushed me with Your vast knowledge. If I am insightful, it is because You have extended a tiny portion of Your sight to me. If I persevere, it is because You hold me up and deflect my enemies from before me.

Oh lover of my soul, I sing Your praises. I glorify Your might. Never let me forget the awesome manifestations of Your greatness. With but a sweep of Your hand, You created the universe. With but a word, You produced enough light to fill the skies with buckets full of sunshine. With the power of Your love, You took on the frailty of mankind.

Bring that love into my soul today. Let me feel Your light. Expose me to Your creativity. Come sit with me and speak Your wisdom to my spirit. Envelop me in Your sweetness. Allow me to feel Your presence in a deeper dimension. Just as You commanded the waters to flow over the earth, wash over me. Purge me. Mold me. Heal me. Do with me as You wish. I am Yours.

Amen.

Blessed are those who dwell in your house;
they are ever praising you.
PSALM 84:4

My Holy Father,

How happy and fortunate I am—how blessed to dwell in Your presence. I am in awe that You chose me. You could live anywhere in the wide expanse of the universe and beyond, but You chose to make my heart Your home until that day when I can come live in Your house. I am humbled and awed by Your confidence in me.

Your promise is almost too wonderful for me. I can only respond by constantly praising Your name. When I see Your mighty power and watch Your exciting plans for my life unfold before me, I cannot remain silent. I must speak out. I must find words to thank You for taking time to work in one such as me. Accept my praises, most high God. Allow me to sing a song of praise in chorus with all those who belong to Your family—all those who have opened the door of their hearts to You. Together we will raise our voices to honor and exalt Your name. Together we will be ever praising You.

I delight to dwell in Your presence, Lord. Thank You for making that possible through Jesus Christ my Lord and Savior. Because of Him, I will sing praises to Your name all day long!

Amen.

The beginning of wisdom is the fear of the LORD,
and knowledge of the Holy One is understanding.
PROVERBS 9:10 NAB

Loving Father,

I have so often put my faith in the pressing matters of this world. *Surely*, I thought, *I will always do well and live life on my own terms*. I believed in my power to control my job, my finances, other people. How foolish I must have seemed to You. Then those certainties began to crumble like the shifting sands which dissolve with the first crashing wave that hits the shore. I felt the waves wash over me, pulling me out into a sea of uncertainty.

But, Lord, I should have known that You would be there! Through my losses, You began to teach me that all my answers reside in You. Even then, I lacked wisdom; for I knew You only with my mind. I could quote Your words and teach from Your parables, but still, I did not understand Your ways.

Now I see that I must know You with my whole heart. I see that my pride is false and I have no strength in myself. I am ready to fully surrender to Your loving care—to depend on You for every need in my life. I will trust in You to still the troubled sea around me and place my feet on solid ground.

Amen.

When times are good, you should be cheerful; when times are bad, think what it means.
ECCLESIASTES 7:14 CEV

Lord,

I have seen both good and bad in my lifetime. Both are powerful and life-changing. But the truth is, that I have never really understood either one. It has taken me a long time to realize that I don't have to understand the reason for everything. It is Your job to know all the "whys." Mine is to be joyful when times are good and ask for wisdom and strength to endure when times are hard. You have even taught me that my difficulties help me appreciate the blessings You have poured out on my life.

When I lost my son, You were there to comfort me and assure me that the dark days would not last forever. Now, at last, I can see sunshine through the pain. You are indeed faithful. And I gain strength from knowing that Your hand is always on my life and the lives of those I love.

My heart is filled with love for You, Lord, and I thank You for Your great faithfulness to me. I will be happy in the good times You bring to my life; and even when the dark clouds park overhead, I will stop to consider Your faithfulness and loving care.

Amen.

Do not arouse or awaken love until it so desires.
SONG OF SONGS 2:7

Lord,

I took a walk today and saw children waiting for the school bus. Some short, some tall. Some squatty and round, others lanky and thin. Laughing, pushing, talking, playing. All precious to You.

I also saw a girl, barely a teenager, holding a tiny bundle. A wiggly bundle. A little baby boy. I smiled at her, Lord. And the young mother shyly smiled back. Yet my heart ached. She was barely more than a child herself. How will she meet the demands that are sure to come from becoming a parent too early in life? And what about the young man responsible for fathering this sweet, wiggly bundle? I wonder if anyone told them that Your instruction to remain pure until marriage was meant to protect them rather than frustrate them.

I know I've failed, Lord. I haven't spoken strongly enough to the children I know and love. I didn't want to appear "old-fashioned." Forgive my silence. Help me to find a way to impress upon the hearts of the children in my life how important it is to find the courage and the commitment to save their passions and love for marriage. And show me how I can help these young ones achieve this righteous goal.

Amen.

Then I heard the voice of the L*ORD* *saying,*
"Whom shall I send? And who will go for us?"
And I said, "Here am I. Send me!"
ISAIAH 6:8

My Lord,

I know so little about Your purpose for my life, but I am certain that You have a perfect plan. Teach me never to hesitate when I hear Your voice. It is my desire to learn to trust You completely, so I am quick to obey and sure to be ready for every step along the path. Whether You send me to far away places or to my neighborhood or workplace, I pray that You will help me to be vigilant, always ready to do what You ask of me.

My talents and abilities are small and imperfect, but they are Yours to use. Give me opportunities to demonstrate Your love to others. Help me never to let my heart grow cold or apathetic, but let me always be ready to do as You ask. Guide my steps, and use my life to bless others. That is my greatest desire.

When I think of the many ways You have blessed my life—both large and small—I am overwhelmed with a sense of thankfulness. Your wonderful gifts of salvation, grace, and unconditional love were given to me freely. How much more, then, must I give myself freely to You?

Amen.

Stand at the crossroads and look; ask for the ancient paths, ask where the good way is, and walk in it, and you will find rest for your souls.

JEREMIAH 6:16

Gracious God,

As I make the difficult decisions each day demands, I take comfort in knowing that Your direction is mine for the asking. It's a good thing, too, because the world You created is a very big, very complicated place. Fortunately, I can always turn to You for guidance.

You know which path is best for me. You hold the vision of what I can accomplish, of what I can contribute to the wonder of Your world. And You know where I need to go to make my contributions. I know the journey won't always be easy. I might find myself on wide, well-lit streets with lots of fellow travelers; but I may also have to brave some narrow, deserted, winding roads where it's impossible to see what's around the next corner.

So as I face today's uncertainties, I am asking, Lord, that You help me to seek Your will in all things. I am asking that You guide me to make choices that will honor and glorify You. I am asking for the strength to be unwavering in my faith. And I am asking for the peace that comes with knowing that, no matter what the next mile brings, I am walking life's roads side by side with You.

Amen.

It is of the LORD'S *mercies that we are not consumed, because his compassions fail not.*
They are new every morning: great is thy faithfulness.
LAMENTATIONS 3:22,23 KJV

Father,

Sometimes I hear myself lamenting like Jeremiah; but then, like him, I remember that I have hope in You and in Your abundant mercy. I remember that You look down on me with compassion. You love me and reach out Your hand to help me in the midst of my problems. Even when I'm whining about troubles I have brought upon myself, You are still there. I feel safe in knowing You will always be nearby, Lord, to give me light, sight, and understanding. Teach me Your ways, I pray, and give me Your wisdom.

I don't trust myself, except under Your care, Lord. What I do trust is Your faithfulness. I will expectantly wait on You, my faithful Father. I will hopefully wait for You, and I will follow after You. And, of course, I'll be asking and asking—always needing and wanting.

Thank You for loving me in spite of my flaws. Thank You for understanding me even when I am incomprehensible to myself. Your mercies are new every morning, and I depend on them. Thank You, Father, for being so good to me. I praise You for Your great faithfulness to me!

Amen.

I will give them an undivided heart and put a new spirit in them;
I will remove from them their heart of stone and give them a heart of flesh.
EZEKIEL 11:19

My Heavenly Father,

Through the years, I've grown to appreciate all the amazing gifts You've given me. But daily life has taken a toll, and I sometimes find myself weighed down by the world. I've wondered what might allow me to regain the openness and exuberance I enjoyed as a child. Now I realize that what I need is a new heart.

This is no small feat, to be sure, but I know all things are possible with You. Just as a skilled surgeon can perform the most delicate of transplants, You can replace my hardened heart. Just as a master craftsman can refurbish a decaying building, You can repair the damages I have sustained. Just as a gifted artist can repaint a fading canvas, You can restore my spirit.

I pray, Lord, that You will give me the courage to open my new heart to those around me, so they can see for themselves the transforming power of Your love. Help me see, with refocused eyes, the grandeur of the world You shaped. And never let me forget to thank You for all You have done.

Amen.

[God] *gives wisdom to the wise and knowledge to the discerning.*
He reveals deep and hidden things; he knows what lies in darkness, and light dwells with him.
DANIEL 2:21,22

Lord God, my God,

I am in awe as I read Daniel's description of You. I feel proud to belong to so great a Father. I get excited when I think about all that You are. I long for revelation of deep and secret things, and Daniel says all revelation comes from You. All light comes from You. All knowledge and understanding come from You.

You are all-powerful. You even rule over the seasons. That must mean You rule the weather! You can set kingdoms up or take them down. Father, in my human weakness, if I forget even a little bit, I begin to be afraid. Like a child losing sight of a parent, I begin to worry. I worry about all the evil I see in the world. Yet my frantic cries quiet as Your Holy Spirit reminds me that You are almighty God, my Creator, You are in charge of the world—everyone and everything in it.

Daniel said that You know what dwells in the darkness, and You bring light. You will use whatever is available for Your purposes. Your ways are so much greater than any I can imagine. I'm so glad they are!

Amen.

Let us acknowledge the LORD; let us press on to acknowledge him.
As surely as the sun rises, he will appear; he will come to us like the winter rains,
like the spring rains that water the earth.
HOSEA 6:3

Never-failing God,

With my whole heart, I acknowledge You as the Lord of my life and hurry to obey You in all I say and do. I proclaim Your faithfulness to me and to all that You have created; for You are as constant as the sun that rises day by day, as certain as the unfolding seasons, and as refreshing as the rains that You send to water the earth.

Your abiding presence fills my heart with gentle confidence and a security of knowing that You will never leave me nor forsake me. As the currents cradle the ocean, so will Your hand sustain me in all of life's ebb and flow. It is in You, oh Lord, that I find what I need for each day. I look to You for my daily sustenance and strength. I rest in the promise of Your unfailing mercy. I acknowledge that You are always at work in my life, bringing all things to pass, each one in its proper time.

I lift my heart to You, a gift of praise. Fill it with Your love and help me proclaim Your greatness to all those who will cross my path today.

Amen.

Return to the L*ORD your God, for he is gracious and compassionate,*
slow to anger and abounding in love, and he relents from sending calamity.
JOEL 2:13

Lord God,

It is good for me to always remember my constant need of You. I can really "blow it" sometimes. When, for example, I offend someone, I so often hesitate to make things right because I fear a negative response. I certainly don't have to fear that from You, Lord. You are always gracious and compassionate, expecting the best from each person.

When someone offends me, the first thing I think about is how to retaliate. But not You. You are always slow to anger and full of forgiveness. It is so good to know that if I should neglect or even disobey, You will discipline me, but You will continue to call me Your son. When I'm genuinely sorry about an offense toward You, God, You will even avert calamity and give me an outcome that I do not deserve.

It's always best to return to You, no matter what I've done or how badly I think I've behaved. For I know that You will always offer open arms to me and accept me as I am. You forgive me and wipe away my tears. You provide the guidance I need so I can become the person You've created me to be.

Amen.

Seek good, and not evil, that ye may live.
AMOS 5:14 KJV

Heavenly Father,

Reading Amos struck up such a cry for help in me. Our little ones, our grandchildren, have a constant exposure to evil. It reaches into every part of our society. It confronts us in every area of our lives, even what we call entertainment.

Dear God, teach us ways to protect ourselves and those who depend on us from being desensitized to human suffering. Help me be the grandmother who seeks good—to find it, talk about it, walk in it, and show it to my grandchildren. I want to point out beauty and good to them. Give their parents wisdom to develop in them soft, caring hearts. Help them, Father, to build courage in their characters that will enable them to stand against evil. Give my children and their children knowledge and wisdom to establish judgment in the gates (our government).

Please, Lord God, be gracious to us and our offspring. Teach us to love goodness rather than evil. Teach us to demonstrate Your character and imitate Your Spirit rather than the spirit that dwells in this world. Help me to bless my children and my grandchildren by speaking the truth in love and being a careful watchman on the wall. And thank You, Lord, for reminding me that the evil in this world will never overtake me because I belong to You.

Amen.

"Though you soar like the eagle and make your nest among the stars,
from there I will bring you down," declares the LORD.
OBADIAH 4

Precious Lord,

I long to be safe and secure within Your loving arms. Don't let me soar to the heights of conceit where I find hope in what I gain, nor stray from Your precious side. But cast me down from any lofty nest into which I rise. Rescue me from vanity, and form within me an humble soul.

So awesome are Your tender mercies and so wide are Your hovering wings. They watch over me when I wander afar and bring me down low to see You face to face; they immerse me in Your love. Keep me from the sharp claws of pride, Lord, when I run and pursue my own ways. Before I fall from Your mindful care, let Your chastisement correct my path and send me running away from evil.

Let me make no room for haughtiness, nor forsake Your goodness and grace. Though I may sit among the stars, cause me to rest at Your feet with my heart outpoured, a broken vessel waiting expectantly for every word You speak. Though I fly with the eagles, I look to You to keep me from harm. Draw me into Your eternal refuge, where I will give You glory and praise. I am blessed by Your radiant presence, to dwell securely forevermore.

Amen.

In my distress I called to the LORD, *and he answered me.*
From the depths of the grave I called for help,
and you listened to my cry.
JONAH 2:2

Father,

I've got problems. Big problems. Ugly problems that have swallowed me up. I feel like I've fallen into a bottomless grave. Though I raise my head, I am only able to see a tiny pinpoint of light in the midst of the darkness. Is that light You? Are You up there? Do You even see me?

In the deepest fathom of my soul, Lord, I do know that You see me. Forgive my doubting. Help me feel Your presence in the midst of this dark night. Don't let me be defeated, despite the hopelessness of this situation. Never let me lose sight of You. Give me the supernatural strength I need to cling to You. Help me to come through these gut-wrenching problems with a deeper knowledge of Your holiness, a broader understanding of Your wisdom, a grander perception of Your love.

And one day, Lord, may I say with confidence that I'm thankful for this long night; that because of the darkness, I learned—I trusted—I grew. Show me, Father, what You want me to see. Don't let this opportunity for growth be wasted by my groaning impatience. Give me You, oh Lord. And let my untrained heart come to see that You are enough—more than enough!

Amen.

What does the LORD *require of you? To act justly*
and to love mercy
and to walk humbly with your God.
MICAH 6:8

Holy Father,

What gift should I bring as I come before You? Will You Who are an eternal Spirit be satisfied with temporal, material things? I wonder if all the earth's treasure could purchase one thing that You need or even desire. For that very reason, I give You my heart—a temple not built with human hands.

Thank You, oh Lord, for teaching me what is good and what You require of me. You would have me act justly in all my dealings. You would have me love others in the same way that I have been loved. You would have me love mercy and show compassion to others, just as You have shown it to me. You would have me humble myself and submit my will to Yours, so I might walk safely and securely and fulfill Your plan for my life.

Thank You, Lord, for making Your will known to me so I can do those things that please You. Thank You for revealing to me Your way so I can choose to follow it. Thank You for giving me Your Spirit to empower me so I can live in harmony with my fellow man: practicing justice, loving mercy, and walking humbly with You.

Amen.

The LORD *is slow to anger and great in power;*
the LORD *will not leave the guilty unpunished.*
NAHUM 1:3

Merciful Father,

You are slow to anger, and I am so quick to become angry. Help me to slow down and take time to properly evaluate a situation before I respond strictly on the basis of my feelings. Help me to see past my own pain and consider the suffering of others. I praise You because You are slow to anger when it comes to my own shortcomings and sin against You.

Oh Lord, teach me to be just and righteous like You. I define justice in such self-serving ways. That is why I fall into anger's trap. I have so much to learn. I want to leave the punishment of the guilty to You. I want to be reminded that Your desire is for every person to come to know You—You approach every situation with redemption in mind.

Remind me of the times that I have had to depend upon Your mercy, Lord. When I become indignant and haughty, speak to my heart and let me feel Your corrective hand on my life. I want to be pleasing in Your sight. I want be more like You each and every day. Thank You for showing me that there is power and protection in self-control.

Amen.

LORD, I have heard of your fame; I stand in awe of your deeds, O LORD. Renew them in our day, in our time make them known.
HABAKKUK 3:2

Almighty God,

I really feel like I am beginning to know You. And the more I know about You, the more I realize how well You know me. You know my hours of certainty, but You also know my moments of doubt. You know that I'm troubled by the things I see in the world today.

Age-old animosities prevent full cooperation and trust between nations. Cities struggle with overcrowding and crime. Families are torn apart by abuse, and children suffer from poverty and neglect. The problems sometimes seem insurmountable. But then I am reminded that You are the solution.

I pray, Lord, that You will remind others of Your presence in the world. I pray that countries in conflict will be shown ways to respect their differences. I pray that those in positions of authority in our cities will experience a reawakening of Your love. I pray that parents and their children will feel the touch of Your Spirit in their lives. And I pray, Lord, that despite my momentary fears or doubts, You will help me live my life fully and with abundant joy; so it will be evident to everyone I meet that I know You.

Amen.

Seek the LORD, all you humble of the land, you who do what he commands.
ZEPHANIAH 2:3

Lord of All,

There is no one who can comfort and deliver like You. My heart is encouraged as I begin to meditate on Your goodness and faithfulness. My life is truly in Your hands, my loving Father. As a child I come to You and rest in Your wisdom. There is nothing in this world that can compare with You. Your presence in my life is the greatest love I have ever experienced. I declare to all the earth that there is no one like You. Guide my life to the destiny and purpose You have ordained

Lord, I gaze at Your creation and long to know You better. I consider Your words of love and comfort and desire to come closer into Your presence. Thank You for paying the price so I can call You Father. I humble my heart before You, my Lord. Speak to me like a soft breeze, that I may know Your will.

Lord, help me to carefully follow all Your instructions so that I may realize all the plans You have for me. I want to glorify You in all that I do. Lord of all, when my heart searches for You, I am never disappointed.

Amen.

"The glory of this present house will be greater than the glory of the former house," says the LORD Almighty.
HAGGAI 2:9

Most Gracious Lord,

I seek to fellowship with You. My foremost desire is for You to abide deep within me and make me Your chosen vessel. I covet this secret and hidden place with You, through which I may walk and gaze upon Your imminent glory. I ask that the chamber of my heart might be cleansed and made holy by Your presence and the fullness of Your radiance.

Establish Your rule and reign within me, Lord. I surrender to You and Your work of grace in my life. Transform me and build me up as a house that is worthy to show forth Your presence in the earth—not a house made of silver and gold, but one that is perfect and holy because Your Spirit dwells there.

Send me forth with lips touched and filled with the fire from Your altar. Mold and form me to show forth Your handiwork. Glorify this present house, my heart, that I might release Your divine revelation in these final days and shake the heavens and the earth with Your manifested glory and praise before You return for those who love You.

Amen.

"Not by might nor by power, but by my Spirit," says the LORD Almighty.
ZECHARIAH 4:6

Dearest Father,

I am so limited and weak. Therefore, it is a great comfort to know that all good things are initiated by You and accomplished by Your Spirit. He gives me the strength I need to overcome the obstacles in my life. His presence within me fills me with great hope and expectation.

Thank You for Your amazing promises and for the wonderful gift of Your Holy Spirit, my everyday Comforter. He helps me to have the proper attitude and spirit and gives me the desire and courage to do what is right. He urges me to speak when the time is right and keep quiet when it is time to listen. He heals me and gives me peace so strong that fear flees from my presence. He makes me better than I am and encourages me to become all that You have ordained me to be.

I know I have no real power in myself. I am dependent on Your Spirit working freely within me. Open my heart, Lord. Cleanse me and make me a fit vessel for Your Spirit. I pray that I will always be submissive to Your will so that my life will reflect Your nature to those around me.

Amen.

I the LORD do not change.
MALACHI 3:6

Unchanging Father,

Thank You, Lord, for Your steadfastness. I can trust You, knowing that You will accept me and show me mercy today the same way You did yesterday and all the days that have gone before. You will always be here supporting me and leading me along the right path. You will never let me down.

I need that stability. Sure, I have good friends and a loving family who have stood by me in good times and bad. But eventually, they will let me down (after all, they are only human and suffer the same inconsistencies that I do). But You are as steady as a rock, as constant as the North Star—always loving me, always forgiving me, always pushing me to grow. Thanks for being here with me, for being the One Who does not change.

Of course, I know that means Your standards don't change either. You want me to be righteous and compassionate, just like You. Forgive my fickleness—the times I have ignored You or downright disobeyed You. Give me the courage to commit myself to You wholeheartedly. Grant me the constancy of character that You have shown to me. Help me to be the kind of person You can depend on to show love and mercy to others.

Amen.

Ye are the light of the world. A city that is set on an hill cannot be hid.
MATTHEW 5:14 KJV

Dear Heavenly Father,

I know that all light comes from You—sun, moon, and stars—even the elements by which a candle burns. You, Lord, are the greatest, truest light of all! Teach me to be a child of the light, Your Own true daughter, bringing Your light to those who dwell in darkness.

As I kneel here praying, I see a light shining from the mountaintop across the valley. It sets up on a hill, so it is easily seen. Even though it is no stronger than those in the valley below, its position keeps it from being shrouded and allows it to serve as a beacon for those below. In the same way, Father, use me. Give me the courage to stand alone on the hill, shining the light of Your love on those searching for truth. Give me the strength to keep my vigil without complaining or compromising, standing firm in all types of weather, that others might find their way.

Oh Lord, if this world ever needed illumination it is now. Rekindle me, Your child. Let my light shine for You. Fill me always with Your Holy Spirit, for only then can I truly shine!

Amen.

What good is it for a man to gain the whole world, yet forfeit his soul?
MARK 8:36

Yes, Lord,

It was wrong, but not so terribly wrong. It's not my fault that the cashier undercharged me. Why should I go to the trouble of pointing it out when it was her mistake. It's not like I set out to cheat anyone. Surely You wouldn't hold that against me, Lord.

Help me to see the big picture, Lord. Help me to always remember that my integrity can be destroyed a little bit at a time. Make me as vigilant in the small things as I am in the big things. Help me to remember that Your flawless character is to be my example rather than the flaws and shortcomings of my own sinful justifications. Showing love, generosity, and grace to my fellow humans should be my focus. Keep reminding me that my soul is what is at stake—not just for eternity, but for the here and now.

Bring me to a place of scrupulous honesty and abundant love for others, Lord. Help me to find the peace that comes from knowing I have done what is right whether anyone ever knows it or not. Thank You, Lord, for grace and forgiveness.

Amen.

There is rejoicing in the presence of the angels of God over one sinner who repents.
LUKE 15:10

My Awesome Redeemer,

You are a celebrating God. Nothing excites Your eternal heart quite so much as a homecoming. That's what repentance is all about to You, bringing a lost person home. All Your power, all Your love, all Your mercy focus on that one mission. But I was wondering, Lord, are there ever moments of silence when no one repents? What pain there must be in that emptiness.

It is my desire, Lord, to celebrate with You and to grieve with You. Let my heart fill with joy when I see someone come home to You. And when I see no one coming, let the pain I feel push me to spread Your message to those around me. Help me feel the pulse of Your great heart as it beats for repentance and homecomings, precious Father. Help me to join Your mission every day, to seek the lost and celebrate the found.

And once I am in tune with Your heart—once I have experienced in small part the anguish and celebration that You feel over one single soul—then, oh Lord, I pray that the pain and the joy I feel will serve as a constant reminder of the faithful and constant love You have poured out on me.

Amen.

Love one another. As I have loved you, so you must love one another.
By this all men will know that you are my disciples, if you love one another.
JOHN 13:34,35

Oh Lord, my Father,

What a difficult command You have given us. Loving one another is difficult enough at times, but can we ever love one another as You have loved us? Are we even capable of such love? You gave Your very life for me, Lord. How could I ever love another as much as that? I doubt that I could ever love one so purely and grandly.

It is easy for me to love those who love me first, those who are good to me and treat me fairly. But, Lord, You loved even Your enemies. How amazing that is to me! You gave Your life for us while we were still sinners. Can I die like You did? Can I put to death the part of me that wants to be admired and respected, praised and prized? Is this what You require?

Help me to love as You love, Father. Help me to follow Your example, remembering that You do not love only when You have time or only when it is easy. You love us with a pure heart, expecting nothing in return. Help me to love others until it hurts, until it costs, until I love like You.

Amen.

Salvation is found in no one else,
for there is no other name under heaven given to men by
which we must be saved.
ACTS 4:12

Dearest Lord Jesus,

You are the seed Who willingly fell from the bough of the tree and risked the perils of this wilderness we know as earth to become "the true Vine." Through all the splinters and thorns, the whips and the scorns, You pressed on to rescue us, to provide us with hope—the only means of hope in a hopeless world. Instead of leaving me to perish, to wither away into dust, You planted life in my heart.

Thank You for making me a branch on Your vine and for giving me eternal life. Thank You for making a way for me to come to You without fear of being turned away. My heart is full of praise for You and all the things You have done for me. Thank You for loving me enough to give Your life for me.

Though the earth may quake at its very core and the universe rebel against me, I will rejoice because I know that this bond cannot be shaken. It is steady, unbreakable; for it was created by You. You alone are worthy of my praise. There are no other gods who can stand before You.

Amen.

For all have sinned and fall short of the glory of God.
ROMANS 3:23

My Lord,

Your truth reminds me of what I do not want to remember. I feel so guilty for my sin, and it does not make me feel better to be reminded that I am included in "all." It saddens me to think how far we, as a human race, have drifted away from You in our sin. And to think I am a part of that irresponsible group is almost more than I can bear.

My tears flow down my face, springing like a fountain from a broken heart. On my knees, I remain in this state—until I read a little further in Your Book. I hear Paul's reminder that You, oh Christ, "died to sin once for all" (Romans 6:10). That is a part of "all" that makes me rejoice.

The brokenness of the human condition that leads me to sin need not bind me in sorrow forever. You, oh Christ, have died to release me from bondage, not over and over; but one, very effective time—and not just for a few, but for the same "all" who have sinned and fallen short of Your glory. That good news raises me from my repentant knees and causes me to rejoice in the freedom of Your forgiving grace.

Amen.

No eye has seen, no ear has heard,
no mind has conceived what God has prepared
for those who love him.
1 CORINTHIANS 2:9

Loving God,

How often have I ambled through life trying to fool You. I've thought, *If I say my prayers and put my money into the church collection basket, surely You will know I am good and reward me.* Then, how surprised I have been when the rewards have passed me by. Still, I have tried new ways to get Your approval.

But today as I kneel in prayer, I hear You say, "Give Me your heart, my child, and I will do great things for you and through you. Allow Me to guide your steps and then you will find success in all that you do."

So Lord, even now I release all that I am to Your precious Spirit. I trust You with my questions and believe that You will bring me the answers. I trust You with my decisions and believe that You will help me make the right choices. I trust You with my dreams and believe that they will only become bigger and bolder once I have relinquished them into Your outstretched hand. Thank You, Lord, for allowing Your Spirit to live in me.

Amen.

We are hard pressed on every side, but not crushed; perplexed, but not in despair;
persecuted, but not abandoned; struck down, but not destroyed.
2 CORINTHIANS 4:8,9

Mighty God,

I must admit that I get discouraged. I try to maintain a cheerful countenance in the face of hopelessness or antagonism, but sometimes I fail. Surely You know how I feel when I'm confronted with a mean look. It's not always easy to respond in love. You know best about human nature—not only did You create us, but You experienced what it is like to be human. You created my sensitive constitution and designed my emotions. You, more than anyone, are aware of my limitations.

I'm reminded of You, my Savior, Who in the days of Your earthly existence, endured such scorn and ridicule from Your oppressors. I'm not always sure why we humans suffer, but I know that You can identify with me when I feel persecuted. You endured such hostility and overcame. Therefore, I will overcome.

Grant me the strength to hold up under stress. Deliver me from pressures that are too great for me to bear. And I also ask, Lord, that You would grant me grace to bear those responsibilities I can handle, knowing that they will make me stronger. Thank You, Lord, for seeing me through it all.

Amen.

I have been crucified with Christ and I no longer live, but Christ lives in me.
GALATIANS 2:20

Ever-living God,

Within the pages of the Bible, I have learned that it was never Your plan that we should live our lives according to a set of rules and regulations. Instead, You ask us to place our trust in Your Son, Jesus Christ. He lived the perfect life of which we are incapable and then took the punishment for our failures in advance. He did all that so we could shine as living examples of Your mercy and grace.

Thank You, Lord, for the gift of Your Son, Jesus, Who came to this earth to do for me what I could not do for myself. I have placed my trust in Him and accepted Your offer of life everlasting—life in all its abundance.

Because of my identification with Christ, I have been crucified with Him, so it is no longer I who live, but Christ Who lives in me. The new life I now live in the body, I live by faith in Your Son, Who loved me and gave Himself for me. Knowing all this, there is nothing left for me to do but to thank You and give You my praise. It is the honest praise of one who knows who he was and rejoices in who he has become.

Amen.

He chose us in him before the creation of the world to be holy and blameless in his sight.
EPHESIANS 1:4

Gracious Father,

Thank You for all the spiritual blessings that are mine because of my faith in Your Son, Jesus Christ. In Him, I am blessed beyond measure. You chose me before the creation of the world to be holy and blameless in Your sight, knowing that I could only accomplish that as I put my faith in You. You predestined me to be adopted as Your child. That was Your will.

Thank You, Lord, for Your mercy, which You have freely poured out on me. You have forgiven me and redeemed me from all my messes and disastrous choices. So now I can fully enjoy the richness of Your grace. You have made known to me Your plan for my life—a plan that will bring me hope and peace and cannot fail.

Thank You for choosing me to be part of this glorious plan. Because I have trusted in You, I have been marked with a seal, the Holy Spirit, as a guarantee of my spiritual inheritance. What can I give You in return for all these marvelous gifts? I can offer You nothing more and nothing less than my praise and thanksgiving.

Amen.

He who began a good work in you will carry it on to completion until the day of Christ Jesus.
PHILIPPIANS 1:6

Dearest Father,

Help me know the difference between Your work and my sorry attempts to be good or do good. Help me recognize the good work of salvation that forgives, cleanses, redirects, redeems, refines, and reshapes me so Your name is inscribed on my life like an artist's on one of his masterpieces. Nevertheless I think of myself as a work in progress.

Lord, I do want to be like You. While I litter my life with unfinished projects and half-worked-on attitudes, You come with a promise to finish what You start. To that my heart cries, oh Lord, finish me. Help me understand that when I insist on my own way, I tie Your hands. When I try to be good on my own, I present myself unfinished and undone. Where I have substituted my work for Yours, forgive me. Where I have interfered with my ideas or timing, correct me. Help me to follow You so that one day Your work in me will be finished.

I submit to Your hand on my life, Lord. I surrender my hopes and dreams and plans to Your perfect will. Help me always to allow Your good work to accomplish Your perfect will in my life.

Amen.

Set your minds on things above, not on earthly things.
COLOSSIANS 3:2

Heavenly Father,

As I pass from day to day on this journey, please help me stay focused on You. If every thought is entwined with Your Spirit, my walk here will be one of peace and joy. There can be no strife or contention if I will only concentrate on the love and grace You so freely give.

It's hard to imagine how You could love Your children so completely that You would send Your beloved Son to be part of this imperfect world. And how could You send Your Spirit to dwell in my imperfect heart? When I think about how He guards my heart and fills my mind with the understanding of Your Word, I give thanks and praise. He is such a gentle teacher, Lord. His lessons give me unquestioned paths to walk, blameless words to speak, and complete confidence in my thinking. I know Whose child I am, how I am to live and where and how I am to spend eternity. What more could I want than to know You and trust in Your perfect plan?

Father, please help me to give You my first thought in the morning and my last thought in the evening. I realize, the only way my life can be fulfilled and happy is if I turn my thoughts to You, every moment of the day.

Amen.

May God himself, the God of peace, sanctify you
through and through.
May your whole spirit, soul and body be kept blameless
at the coming of our LORD *Jesus Christ.*
1 THESSALONIANS 5:23

God of Peace,

I give You thanks because You have called me to lead a life of peace and holiness. Since I cannot do this in my own strength, I call upon You, knowing that through the power of Your Holy Spirit You will help me to be and do all that You desire.

Like Paul, I know that in me—that is, in my flesh—there dwells no good thing. But also like Paul, I know that the life I now live, I no longer live in the flesh, but in the Spirit. Help me to be more attuned to Your Holy Spirit so I can become more conformed to the image and nature of Jesus, in Whom I have placed my faith and hope.

Lead me, oh Lord, in the paths of righteousness for Your name's sake. Preserve me from evil and keep me from the sin that so easily besets me, so that I may walk in peace, holiness, and newness of life. And by Your Spirit, I ask that You would keep me blameless until that day when I see You face to face. All this I ask through Jesus Christ my Lord.

Amen.

May our LORD Jesus Christ himself and God our Father,
who loved us
and by his grace gave us eternal encouragement and good hope,
encourage your hearts and strengthen you in every good deed
and word.

2 THESSALONIANS 2:16,17

Father God,

Whenever I'm blue and in need of encouragement, I remind myself of Your infinite wisdom and unchanging love for me. At times, however, it's hard for me to see that You are working on my behalf—even though I know Your hand is ever present upon my life, guiding and supporting me, ready to encourage me when I need it most.

When I was twelve, I remember how desperately I wished for a metallic gold bicycle with tinseled streamers flowing from the hand grips. At night I couldn't sleep, for I could only lie there and dream of pedaling that wonderful bike along the sidewalks of my neighborhood. I reminded You so often that I seldom spoke of anything else. But when it didn't come quickly, I thought You had not heard or didn't care.

Back then I couldn't see the wisdom of waiting. I didn't understand the gift of patience and the virtue of hope. Then came the surprise. I received that gold bike for Christmas. It was one of the happiest moments in my life. Thank You, Father, for giving me what I now realize was more than just a great bike.

Amen.

Watch your life and doctrine closely. Persevere in them,
because if you do,
you will save both yourself and your hearers.
1 TIMOTHY 4:16

Dear God,

I've blown it. And my sin has not only affected me and my relationship with You, but also those who saw me. Oh Lord, please forgive me. Pour Your righteousness into my aching soul. Help me get past this disobedience, and restore my right relationship with You.

And as for those who saw my sin, those whom I have affected, give me the courage to make restitution. In all honesty, God, I want to just pretend nothing happened, show up with a smile, and brush this sin under the carpet. But in my spirit I see that is the easy route. The coward's way out. Not the route to holiness.

I beseech You for the courage to take the route to holiness, the valiant road. And once I say my "I'm sorrys," don't let me forget the lesson I've learned. I desperately want to make an impact on the world—for good and not for evil. Don't let me be the person who causes someone else to be lost. Rather, continue to refine me until those watching see less of me and more of You. Curb my stubborn nature. Correct my tongue. Cleanse my wrong attitudes. Carve me into Your image. Make me new.

Amen.

God did not give us a spirit of timidity,
but a spirit of power, of love and of self-discipline.
2 TIMOTHY 1:7

Perfecter of my Faith,

Lord, when I feel inadequate to do what You ask, remind me that I am not my own, but Yours; and because I am Yours, I no longer have to rely on my resources—my courage or eloquence—but I am supplied with the likeness of Your Own character.

There is nothing in the appearance of a tulip bulb to attract attention. Yet when nurtured with water and sunlight, that bulb becomes a radiant expression of Your creativity. A tulip stands tall, confident in the beauty it displays. As You shower special talents into my life and paint me with the radiance of Your character, help me to be a confident exhibit of Your salvation. May I stand with the quiet assurance that You are powerful enough to display in my weakness the majesty of Your unsurpassable love.

I wonder, God, does a butterfly, once it has emerged with splendid wings, still struggle with seeing itself as a common worm? Does it ever return to crawling once it is blessed with the freedom to soar? Lord, remind me of my identity that is found in You. Help me exercise the discipline of striving to match my heart to Your Own so that Your glory may be evident to everyone I meet.

Amen.

In your teaching show integrity, seriousness and soundness of speech that cannot be condemned, so that those who oppose you may be ashamed
because they have nothing bad to say.
TITUS 2:7,8

Lord of Truth,

I am amazed and grateful to think of how, through thousands of years and in hundreds of cultures, You have spoken truth to ordinary people like me. How did You do it? How, in spite of all who misunderstood, denied, or deliberately twisted Your truth, did You keep it pure and accessible?

I know how You did it for me. You brought people into my life who taught me Your ways. People like pastors and professors, who graciously shared their hard-earned knowledge and modeled real piety. There were other teachers, too: my parents, friends, and members of my church family—the cookware salesman, the working moms and housewives, and the sheet metal worker—who taught me with their words and reinforced them with their lives.

Now it's my turn to teach others. Strengthen my will so the truth of my words is proven by the integrity of my character. Help me live a consistent life in front of my children and my spouse, my neighbors, coworkers, and others whom You bring into my sphere of influence. May Your grace and truth compensate for the times I fail to "walk my talk." Thank You again for Your glorious truth and the power it has to change lives.

Amen.

I pray that you may be active in sharing your faith, so that you will have a full understanding of every good thing we have in Christ.

PHILEMON 6

Father God,

What does it mean for me to share my faith? If I tell my neighbor I am praying for her; if I sing on the worship team at church once a month; if after some incident with my five-year-old, I speak of what Your Word has to say, is that sharing my faith?

Lord, I know I'm not someone who can go door-to-door talking to strangers about Your love and forgiveness. Maybe You expect this from some of Your children, but I believe that You have a different plan for me. Please help me slow down. Calm me. I need to be quiet more in order to hear You asking me to offer encouragement to others, to help someone learn a song that will worship You, to live what is right as an example for my children.

When I fail, Lord, as I am sure to do, teach me to model humility and grace. Show me that by displaying these traits, I am most like You. Remind me, Lord, that when I lift You up, You will draw people. It is not dependent upon my charm or boldness or intelligence, it depends solely upon my willingness.

Amen.

Encourage one another daily, as long as it is called Today, so that none of you may be hardened by sin's deceitfulness.
HEBREWS 3:13

Dear Lord of Encouragement,

How many times have I felt that I should pick up the phone or write a quick note of encouragement to a Christian friend? And how many times have these nudges been pushed aside by more pressing issues, such as laundry or dishes? Your Word tells me there may be eternal consequences if I fail to encourage someone today—and every day.

Sincere encouragement makes it easier for people to face difficult circumstances. I want to be part of that process, Lord. Help me not to get so involved in my own agenda that I miss Your still, small voice urging me to step forward and take someone's hand in their time of need.

I know You do not ask me to encourage others simply to assign me another duty. There are benefits for the receiver and the giver. The balm of encouragement allows my heart to remain soft and filled with compassion for those around me. That is not an easy thing in this destructive and self-centered world. Yet it allows me to recognize the good in people and find that my spirit has been lifted, too. Thank You, Lord, for reminding me to encourage others. The dishes can wait—I've got a phone call to make!

Amen.

Every good and perfect gift is from above, coming down from the Father of the heavenly lights.
JAMES 1:17

Father of Lights,

What a title! You are the Father, the Begotten, the Creator of light, of enlightenment. You are the Giver of knowledge and truth. These are true gifts. Understanding. Light. Wisdom. Are these the good and perfect gifts from above?

Wisdom was Solomon's choice when You told him he could ask for anything he wanted from You. What would I have asked? Would I have requested trials to teach me patience and make me mature? Would I have asked for wisdom, for truth, for understanding? Would I have asked for pain to make me gracious and merciful or for tribulation to make my spirit grow strong? I don't think so.

Forgive me, Lord, for being so earthly minded. Forgive me for not seeking wisdom as the priceless treasure Your Word says it is. I have been so overly concerned about my physical well-being that I have rarely considered my spiritual health. Plant in me a desire for the eternal gifts, a desire to find Your light, to search for Your wisdom, to cry out for knowledge and understanding, to seek every good and perfect gift that comes from You. Thank You, Father, for Your love that gives me what I truly need.

Amen.

Do not repay evil with evil or insult with insult,
but with blessings,
because to this you were called so that you may
inherit a blessing.
1 PETER 3:9

Loving Father,

I come to You for help in understanding my world. So many people live by a code of revenge. It's frightening to see a driver cut someone off in traffic and hear the exchange of angry words. Even in our homes, arguments often turn into shouting matches as insult follows insult. How sad for You to witness the ways in which we corrupt our world with negative responses.

Help me to be an agent of change in my world, to make a commitment to dispel angry behavior and positively affect people around me. You have given me all I need to be happy, Lord. Teach me to smile and offer a helping hand instead of angry words. Guide me so my behavior reflects Your love rather than my selfishness.

Loving Father, in Your mercy, teach me that I can't control others, but I can initiate the healing process with what I say and do. Healing must start with me. Help me to be a shining light. Teach me how I can ease the anguish of those whose souls remain shrouded in darkness. Give me the grace to be better than I am, more forgiving, more loving, more caring. I receive it, Lord.

Amen.

His divine power has given us everything we need for life and godliness through our knowledge of him who called us by his own glory and goodness.
2 PETER 1:3

Lord God,

Thank You for calling me to witness Your glory and goodness in my life. It seems unfathomable to me that You have chosen me. It is even more thrilling to realize that You have given me everything I need to live a life worthy of Your great love. You have both chosen me and empowered me for success.

Lord, help me rise up to the challenge You have set before me. Help me become all that You have created me to be. And help me remember that You are my source in every situation—everything I could possibly need to walk in Your perfect will for my life has already been provided. I rejoice in that, and I promise You that I will never take it for granted.

Thank you, Lord, that in Your immeasurable kindness, You called me to life—a life that is full and beautiful because You have revealed Your glory and goodness through Christ. Help me grow in wisdom and, ultimately, in godliness, so that I may make the most of the life You have given me.

Amen.

If we confess our sins, he is faithful and just and will forgive us our sins
and purify us from all unrighteousness.
1 John 1:9

Redeeming Savior,

I am grateful for Your love for me. The challenges of the world sometimes overtake me, cause me to see my need of Your grace. Help me view my shortcomings as opportunities to know You in closer ways. My Lord, I come to You for grace and hope. I am thankful I don't have to figure out life by myself, that even when things press in on every side, I can come to You. You are the God of all hope.

In the midst of my faults, I feel Your love and grace. When I feel like giving up, You are with me, making a way for me to become more like You. Lord, there is none more faithful than You. Your mercies are new every morning—and I am in need of those great mercies as I confess and surrender the darkness in my life.

Wash me, that I may be purified, restored, and renewed. I am growing and changing because You love me, even in my weakness. Let Your Spirit lift me up to where You want me to be, and change my ways. My heart and life are Yours. Thank You for another chance. Help me show others how forgiving, faithful, and powerful You are.

Amen.

Grace, mercy and peace from God the Father and from Jesus Christ, the Father's Son, will be with us in truth and love.

2 JOHN 3

Dear Lord,

Thank You for Your Word that makes the truth so certain and love so sure. Thank You for Your mercy and peace that were brought to me by Your Son—Who made Himself human in order to show me the way to truth through love.

Lord, let me be an ambassador, a spokesman for that great blessing in my generation. I receive it for my children and for myself. I am depending on You to give me the strength and wisdom to direct my decisions—my life. I am looking to You to keep me from straying from the path by always keeping the truth before me. I am resting in Your love, which will never fail.

When I doubt or get confused, Father, I pray You will bring to my remembrance this little letter; and I will be reassured of this mighty truth—that grace, mercy, and peace come from You through the Lord Jesus Christ, Your Son. I am grateful for these words, inspired by Your Holy Spirit to bring me great comfort and joy. Help me to be a source of Your love and truth to those whose lives I touch each day.

Amen.

I pray that you may enjoy good health and that all may go well with you,
even as your soul is getting along well.
3 JOHN 2

Dear Lord,

How grateful I am that You care about the condition of my soul. You have created me so that problems in my soul are reflected in my health and in my emotions. Whatever I plant in the center of my life will most surely spring forth in other areas, providing a garden with awesome potential for both blessing and destruction.

When I do those things that I know are right and my soul is prospering, the garden of my life yields good fruit—kindness, gentleness, mercy, and peace. Help me, Lord, to keep my soul clean and pure toward You, spreading good seed in my life and the lives of those I touch. Keep me, Lord, from those things that encourage weeds capable of choking out the good fruit. And, Lord, keep the soil of my soul turned and ready for the good seed You provide through Your Word and Your example.

As I feed on Your promises, blessings, and commandments, help me to remember that all the good things in my life come from You. Your blessing keeps me on a dependable cycle of planting and harvesting good things. Thank You, Lord, for everything!

Amen.

Keep yourselves in God's love as you wait for the mercy of our LORD Jesus Christ to bring you to eternal life.
JUDE 21

My Faithful God,

As I look around me and see all that is happening in the world, I can't help but believe You will be returning soon. Help me to be ready, Lord, with a clean heart, anticipating the fulfillment of all that is to come. I ask You to help me guard my heart diligently from the distractions that can push me off the path and cause me to miss Your mercy and grace in the times ahead.

Lord, remind me daily to renew my mind by reading Your Word and to pray regularly for strength and courage. Guarding my heart will keep me from succumbing to fear, worry, self-centered thoughts and actions, false doctrines, and any number of other things that would cause me to stumble. Help me to keep my eyes on You and submit myself to Your will and Word.

And Lord, remind me that I am not traveling through this world alone. Let Your light shine so brightly in my heart that it illuminates the darkness around me. There are still so many who have never experienced Your love and mercy. I trust You, Father, because You are ever faithful.

Amen.

"I am the Alpha and the Omega," says the LORD *God,*
"who is, and who was,
and who is to come, the Almighty."
REVELATION 1:8

Holy Father,

It gives me so much comfort to be reminded of Your unwavering presence in the world. Life's changes are never easy, and they can get really scary. There are times when I wonder where I am headed, how I will know when I get there, and if anybody will be there to greet me when I arrive. I draw strength from the certainty that, no matter what else changes in my life, You are forever unchanging.

I know that You will never abandon me or let me down or lose faith in me. Though I may stumble, You will always help me regain my balance. Though I may lose my way, You will guide me safely home again. Though I may get tired, You will give me rest and comfort. Thank You for being the consistency, the true continuity, in my life.

Father, grant me the courage to embrace change, but please also give me the strength to keep change from engulfing me. Help me recognize Your signposts when I see them, and help me have the faithfulness to follow Your lead. And keep reminding me, Lord, that no matter where I go, You will always be waiting to welcome me when I arrive.

Amen.

I am with you and will watch over you wherever you go,
and I will bring you back to this land.
I will not leave you until I have done
what I have promised you.
GENESIS 28:15

Oh God,

How comforting are Your words: "I am with you and . . . I will not leave you." So many times I have felt so alone and scared, overwhelmed by the challenges of my day, and I stopped to remember those precious words. What comfort it brings to know that Almighty God cares that much about me.

I read in the Old Testament how You walked with Noah; how You were a friend to Abraham; how You delivered Joseph from his captivity; and how at even just a morsel of faithfulness on the part of Your people, You protected and led them to safety and prosperity. And, Lord, I know they had to be afraid and overwhelmed; yet, seeing Your faithfulness to them, I know You'll always be faithful to me.

Oh God, my God, stamp my heart with the knowledge of Your faithfulness. Bring to my memory all the prayers You have answered, all the wonders You have shown me. Let me always remember that even when I don't feel like You're with me, You are there. Your presence is not based upon my mere mortal feelings, but rather on Your enduring faithfulness.

Amen.

The LORD, the compassionate and gracious God,
slow to anger,
abounding in love and faithfulness.
EXODUS 34:6

Lord,

I really need a glimpse of Your compassion today. I know that You see every fiber of my soul. And what I'm about to say is no surprise to You . . . but when I fail You, I feel so disgusted with myself. Then I start thinking You must feel the same way.

But, Father, that contradicts everything You are—the God of compassion, of grace, of love, of faithfulness. You are the God Who is slow to anger. Please give me an understanding of Your long-suffering, forgiving nature. Wrap Your arms around me and soothe my agitated soul. I guess, more than anything else, I just need a hug from You today.

Forgive me for doubting Your unconditional love. And as I strive to be more like You, teach me to extend Your mercy to those around me who desperately need You. Don't let me get so focused on my own failures that I am of no use to You. But rather give me a renewed view of the cross, Your outstretched arms, Your compassion, and Your overwhelming love—all flowing to me even in Your time of greatest pain and sorrow. Empower me to radiate that love in such a way that others will ask, that others will want, that others will know.

Amen.

I will walk among you and be your God,
and you will be my people.
LEVITICUS 26:12

Father,

When I first read this verse, it was hard for me to relate this promise You made to the Israelites of long ago to me in this generation. But then I remembered that every believer is one of Your people. I don't have to be a patriarch of the Old Testament or a member of a certain nationality. If I believe and love You, I am Your child.

You will guide me and protect me, redeem me and save me. Your love for me will be as a father's love is for his child. Oh Lord, what a blessing! And to think that You would come into my world, that You would leave that unfathomable place called Heaven to be with me in the midst of my mundane life.

Dear Lord, help me to be worthy of Your presence. Give me integrity in my everyday actions. Help me keep my heart pure and my mind clean. Check me if I wander too far from Your ways. Inspire me to treat all people with respect and love, knowing that we are all Your children. Help me acknowledge Your presence and speak to You as I go through my day, whether it be in the office, the market, at home, or at the playground. Guide me in Your paths of righteousness.

Amen.

Is the LORD'S power limited?
NUMBERS 11:23 NAS

Lord,

By Your power You made the heavens; You made the earth. From the dust of the earth and the breath of Your mouth, You made living, breathing, loving people. How could I ever believe that You would be unable to take care of my needs? Why should I worry? Why should I fret? Nothing is too hard for You.

Thank You for my family, my friends, my coworkers. Thank You for the myriad ways You open the paths around me to share Your love with them. Thank You for a heart that beats with Your vision, Your words, and Your compassion. Thank You for loving me, so that I can love others. I praise You, Lord, for Your boundless provision. Thank You for the food You spread on my table. Thank You for the roof that covers my head at bedtime. Thank You for taking care of the financial needs that sometimes seem to overwhelm me. Thank You for reminding me that everything I have belongs to You, first and foremost.

Thank You, dearest Friend, for Your infinite wisdom that guides me—for Your strength that holds me up when everything around me seems to be crumbling. Thank You that Your power is never limited on my behalf. Find me always faithful in praise for all that You do and all that You are.

Amen.

Know therefore that the LORD your God is God; he is the faithful God, keeping his covenant of love to a thousand generations of those who love him and keep his commands.
DEUTERONOMY 7:9

Faithful Father,

I know that You are God and that there is no other. I know that You are a covenant-keeping God, fulfilling Your Word for generations to those who love You and put their trust in You. I know that not one word of all Your promises to Your people has ever failed.

Thank You, Lord, that to You a thousand years is like a day gone by or like a watch in the night that has passed. You never change; there is not even the shadow of turning in You. You are from everlasting to everlasting, and Your eye is always upon those who submit themselves to You and follow the leading of Your Holy Spirit.

It is so comforting, Father, to know that You are always with me to watch over and take care of me. Day and night my thoughts turn to You in quiet confidence, knowing that whatever may come my way, You are always awake and alert, ever ready to intervene on my behalf. I praise You for Your faithfulness and trustworthiness. You are my strength and my refuge. In You I find peace and rest for my soul.

Amen.

Not one of all the LORD'S good promises to the house of Israel failed;
every one was fulfilled.
JOSHUA 21:45

Lord,

I humbly come before You to apologize for the many broken promises I have made to You. Every promise was an effort to prove my love to You. They were notes, each major and minor, compiled into a song I had not yet learned. A myriad of notes screaming to be released from behind the prison bars of the sheet music. Now I bow down and ask that You teach me to play because Your songs are perfect, and Your promises are true.

Every rainbow I see, whether it comes after a cleansing rainstorm or dances as colorful sun rays into a prism, reminds me that Your promises, unlike so many of mine, are golden—pure and everlasting. They always come to pass. Your promises are the boldness in my speech and the confidence in my walk. They nourish me and bring me life.

I will make one last promise, and I am a fool if I cannot honor it, that I will always believe in the security of Your Word. Where man fails in all his good intentions, You, Jesus, are true to fulfill every letter of Your promises to Your children. You are the explanation for my faith.

Amen.

The LORD will rule over you.
JUDGES 8:23

My Glorious Lord,

Hallowed is the place where You abide, far above all that is and ever shall be. You, Oh Lord, rule supreme over all the wonders of the universe. In Your presence, all creation stands in awe. Your manifested presence overshadows those You love and protects them from the wiles of the evil one. You have enclosed them under the hovering wings of Your grace and mercy. Great are Your ways, oh Lord.

I read in Your Word all authority and power reside in You, and You rule over Your people with goodness and grace. Lord, I know that all my hopes and dreams reside in the kingdom wherein You reign. Therefore, Lord, rule over me. I commit all that I have and all I am to You. Only under Your rule can the peace and joy of Your promises be my possession.

I raise my hands, Lord, as a sign of my full surrender to You. Accept my sacrifice and keep me in the hollow of Your hand. Show me how to be a pleasing citizen of Your kingdom. I am delighted to be found under Your authority because I know that You, oh Lord, rule by love. I receive Your love today and place my hope fully in Your outstretched hand.

Amen.

May the LORD *repay you for what you have done.*
May you be richly rewarded by the LORD,
the God of Israel, under whose wings you
have come to take refuge.
RUTH 2:12

My Rewarder,

I see a pattern at work in Your creation. I see that good deeds are rewarded by goodness in return. I find that peacemakers gain peace for themselves, givers of gifts receive treasures, and the friendly make friends. When I stop to think about it, this principle exists everywhere I look. The stalk of corn in a farmer's field comes directly from the kernel planted in the farmer's soil. The wealth from a rich man's savings is the surplus of his first invested sum.

I am reminded of the simplicity of the rule we call "golden" that describes the law of giving and receiving. It is a divine currency that transcends money, social status, and age. An investment in kindness or consideration always returns rich dividends to the one giving. Anyone can share in the blessings!

As I invest my life, oh Lord, I will look to You for my reward. Grant me the gift that is most precious, the reward most prized—that I might dwell in Your presence all the days of my life. As I receive the reward of Your goodness and grace, I will have even more to invest.

Amen.

There is no Holy One like the LORD;
there is no Rock like our God.
1 SAMUEL 2:2 NAB

Loving Father,

Maine is beautiful in summer. Thanks for sending me there to rest my mind and body. It is so like You to bring spiritual refreshing as well. As I walked each day to the edge of the jagged cliffs and watched the sea crashing against the black rocks, my spirit was touched by the strength and majesty of this curious conflict. For the first time, I considered that the rock resolutely stands firm in the face of the wave's constant battering.

Standing there on the cliffs with the wind sweeping against my face and the mist in my hair, I knew with certainty where I must find my strength. You, Father, are my rock, my fortress against the surging waves. Indeed, You are mightier than the resolute cliffs and the forceful sea. You are my stronghold in times of trouble and the sweet breath of life against my cheek.

This new understanding has brought me renewal and courage to forge ahead with my life, leaving behind my failures and disappointments, and moving on to the challenges and victories You have ordained for me. I know that as I go, I shall step lightly on my path; for I am resting in the shadow of Your greatness, abiding in the safety of Your Spirit. Thank You, Lord.

Amen.

How great you are, O Sovereign LORD!
There is no one like you,
and there is no God but you, as we have heard
with our own ears.
2 SAMUEL 7:22

Oh Lord,

How great You are! Your faithfulness exceeds even our dreams! You not only heal us and protect us, You give us more than we ask for. Our perception of You is so limited by our smallness of understanding, yet You prove Yourself again and again. You do more than we can imagine. You're not only merciful and loving, You're extravagant! Through Your grace You give us more than we deserve. You are not like man who is limited by knowledge and understanding, judgment and emotions. You are God. There is no one like You!

Your glorious works are proclaimed in Scripture, oh Lord. And Your people proclaim Your magnificent deeds as well. They marvel at Your work in their lives—touching hearts, mending relationships, healing broken bodies, and giving peace in the midst of impossible situations.

Receive my praise this day, dear Father. It is to You that I direct my thanksgiving. Open my ears that I might continue to hear of Your great deeds, and touch my lips that I might sing Your praises from dawn to dusk. Heal my heart that I might be found worthy in Your sight, a fit vessel to proclaim Your greatness.

Amen.

O LORD, God of Israel, there is no God like you in heaven above or on earth below—you who keep your covenant of love with your servants who continue wholeheartedly in your way.

1 KINGS 8:23

Heavenly Father,

As King Solomon prayed in the days of the kings of Israel, I pray now in the days when people are ruled by presidents, dictators, and all sorts of governors—some good, some evil. I praise You, Lord, as Solomon did. You are the great God of all the earth, and there is no God like You, not in the heavens above nor on the earth beneath. You keep all Your covenants, and You are merciful to those who walk before You with clean hearts.

Lord, cleanse my heart so that I might walk before You. I praise and thank You for the redemption You have provided for me. You are the same now as You were in Solomon's time. Solomon was praying for the temple he had built for You, honoring the words You had spoken to his father David.

Oh God, now let my heart be Your temple, the dwelling place of Your Holy Spirit. What an awesome plan. The Spirit of the Lord God of all the universe has found His home in the hearts of mere men and women.

Amen.

O LORD, God of Israel, enthroned between the cherubim, you alone are God over all the kingdoms of the earth. You have made heaven and earth.
2 KINGS 19:15

Dear Lord,

Here I am again reading the daily news. As usual, I'm worried and overwhelmed by the crime rate and the threat of war and the uncertain economy. Everywhere I turn, I see nothing but gloom and doom and a dark future. I'm tempted to wring my hands, chew my fingernails, and adopt a general attitude of despair.

But then I remember—as I always do—that You alone are God over all the kingdoms of the earth. You alone know the future. You alone made the heavens and the earth, the very earth I now live on. And You are in control, no matter what.

Oh Father, I don't want to focus on what's wrong with the world. I want to focus on what's right with You. Regardless of what happens around me, sharpen my focus until I see You glorified every hour, every minute, every second of my day. You, just You, and nothing else. Shine Your radiance on my spirit. Purify my heart. Cleanse my mind of the darkness of this world. Teach me to trust You with abandon. Give me peace about the future, which You control. And as I gaze on You, engrave Your very image into my soul.

Amen.

For great is the L*ORD and most worthy of praise;*
he is to be feared above all gods.
1 CHRONICLES 16:25

Almighty God,

I thank You and call on Your name because You are such a good God. Thank You for all the marvelous things You have done for me, all Your wonderful acts on my behalf. I'm awestruck when I think of Your holiness, Lord. I look to Your strength as I face each day. Knowing that You are present is so comforting.

Help me proclaim Your wonders and tell others about Your amazing deeds. Help me tell those whose lives I touch that You are great and worthy of praise, that You are to be feared above all gods. All the gods of this world are nothing, but You, Lord, made the heavens and the earth. You alone have made all that my eyes see. You alone are worthy of great honor!

I give You praise and glory, Father; I give You the honor that is due Your holy name. I worship You in the splendor of Your holiness. With the heavens I rejoice and am glad. In the midst of Your people, I say, "The Lord reigns!" I give thanks to You, holy Father, for You are good, and Your steadfast love endures forever. Praise be to You, Lord, from everlasting to everlasting.

Amen.

For the eyes of the L*ORD* *range throughout*
the earth to strengthen
those whose hearts are fully committed to Him.
2 CHRONICLES 16:9

Oh Lord,

Search my heart and see if I offend You in any way. Am I fully committed to You? Are You sovereign in my heart above my own comfort, success, and belongings? Do I put myself in places of quiet and communion, or am I distracted by the trappings of my everyday life? Did Your gentle whisper get lost in the clutter of my day? Were You talking to me, but I was too busy to hear? Is my life too full of my own agenda?

Shake me, Lord, and bring me to my senses. I want to be consumed with devotion to You. I know Your goodness. I know Your faithfulness. I know the peace You bring in the midst of my doubts, fears, and self-made messes. I know the thrill of Your answers that come to me through Scripture. I love the way Your voice nudges me in the early morning light and at the quietness of dusk. As a mere mortal, I can't comprehend You, but some great day I will see You as You truly are.

Oh Lord, help me in my weakness. Strengthen my heart to be fully committed to You. As You look throughout the earth, let Your eyes fall on me.

Amen.

With praise and thanksgiving they sang to the L*ORD:*
"He is good; his love to Israel endures forever."
EZRA 3:11

Dear Lord,

Praised be Your name, oh Lord Most High, for You are worthy to be praised—on the good days and the bad. Thank You that You are mindful of me even when I am so busy I forget to be mindful of You. You have given me great mercy when I have been forgetful and careless in my acknowledgment of You, my loving Lord.

Thank You for family and friends with whom I can join in singing Your praises. You have given me so much more than I deserve. You have brought me from utter despair into the light of hope and gladness. Thank You for holding my hand when no one else was there, when I was lonely and sad.

The days of my youth are gone, but You have not forsaken me. You have lovingly carried me through many trials and tribulations. Yes, Lord, as with Israel, Your mercy endures for more than a lifetime, for more than a generation. It lasts forever. I am so happy to be able to call You Father. Help me sing and truly praise You, whether alone or with others, because Your supreme sacrifice gives me new life and great hope for the future.

Amen.

Do not grieve, for the joy of the LORD is your strength.
NEHEMIAH 8:10

Oh God of Joy,

It is difficult to celebrate when I see only my flaws and shortcomings. Grief floods my spirit as I come face to face with my failings. When I compare my attitudes and actions with Your perfect standards, I see all too plainly just how short I fall. I can never live up to Your example and expectation of righteousness and holiness.

But You see things differently. You view my feeble attempts to follow You as a joyful reason to celebrate. How is it possible that someone lowly like me can bring pleasure and happiness to the Most High God? Yet You find joy in providing a way of salvation for me. You see my redemption as something to celebrate. You are not pleased when I wallow in despair and grief over my humanity. Instead You rejoice when I cry out for fellowship and communion with You. You long to be with me, too!

Today, I will walk in joy and remember that my strength comes not from my own goodness but from Yours. I will put aside my grieving; for when I grieve, I am focusing only on myself. Instead I will rejoice with You and celebrate Your presence in my life.

Amen.

Who knows but that you have come to royal position for such a time as this?
ESTHER 4:14

My Father,

I am excited and filled with anticipation when I consider that You have placed me on this earth at a certain time for a certain purpose. Don't let me miss Your plan, Lord. Give me the courage to do whatever You set before me and say, as Esther did, "If I perish, I perish" (Esther 4:16). I want to live true to my calling and the purpose for which I was created.

And I pray, Lord, that my children will not miss the purpose for which they were born. I ask You to use me to give direction and encouragement as they look for Your perfect plan. Give me the words that I need to share the principles set forth in Esther's wonderful story—You always give us what we need to do the work You have called us to do.

Open my eyes, Lord, to the assignments You still have ahead for me. I may not be called to speak to a king as Esther was. I may not be called to intervene on behalf of an entire nation as Esther was. But whether I have been called to speak to one or to many, give me Your words, and keep me always in Your perfect will.

Amen.

Blessed is the man whom God corrects; so do not despise the discipline of the Almighty.
For he wounds, but he also binds up; he injures, but his hands also heal.
JOB 5:17,18

Almighty God,

You are the Father of all. Like any loving father, You provide me with all I need to be the best I can be. There are so many things about You, Lord, that amaze me. Your creation confounds my mind—the air that we can't see, being an essential necessity for things that are seen.

Your Word is full of wisdom and revelations that guide my life every day. I love Your Word and the guidance it gives. My life is blessed because of You. Help me learn more of Your ways and give me the strength to live by Your principles.

When I open Your holy Word, I find refuge. When I meditate on Your goodness, I am healed. At times when I am going down the wrong paths in life, Your Word restores me. You restore me unto Yourself. I am assured that I have help in Heaven to live and glorify the Almighty God here on earth. The blessings of Your kingdom are abounding in my life as I am molded and formed in Your love. I love You because You first loved me. Lord, make me more like You.

Amen.

As the deer pants for streams of water, so my soul pants for you, O God.
My soul thirsts for God, for the living God. When can I go and meet with God?
PSALM 42:1,2

Dearest Lord,

My words cannot express the longing in my heart to know You deeply, personally, intimately. You created me with a void that is filled only by being with You. Even before I met You, I knew something was missing in my life. Thank You, Father, for awakening my soul, for drawing me to You.

I love to be in Your presence, Lord. Peace reigns there, and incredible joy. It is there that my every need is met. May I never forget that You are the Source of all life. You are truly the only living God—no one else can satisfy.

Help me, Lord, to see this day as another opportunity for me to encounter You. I will take time to sit with You, to worship You, to commune with You. You created me simply for the joy of knowing me and being known by me. You are my best Friend, my Father, my Provider, and my Salvation. There is no higher calling I can ever achieve than to know You, to praise You through my life. I rest and abide in Your presence today.

Amen.

Glory in his holy name; let the hearts of those who seek the *LORD rejoice.*
Look to the LORD and his strength; seek his face always.
PSALM 105:3,4

To the Most High God,

A seed planted in good soil will grow to bear good fruit. I want to be buried in Your unfailing love. I desire to be a seed growing out of the peace that comes from being one of Your children. Plant me deep so I will be rooted in Your kindness and filled with Your faithfulness, always practicing self-control. I desire to be totally consumed by You.

Holy Father, come to me like a rain after a long drought. I thirst for Your living waters. My branches are raised to celebrate the goodness of Your rains. Every leaf that grows in the fullness of my foliage springs from the joy of knowing You. Always stretching myself toward that great blue sky, I long to look past the clouds and into the gentleness of Your being. You are Lord of the earth and Lord of the high heavens. All that moves, all that lives under the sun, lives only because of Your grace. And if I become uprooted, I know that You will sustain me.

So I continue to praise You, for You are always good to me. Thank You for nurturing me—You have brought forth blossoms I never knew I could produce.

Amen.

He delighteth not in the strength of the horse: he taketh not pleasure in the legs of a man. The LORD taketh pleasure in them that fear him, in those that hope in his mercy.

PSALM 147:10,11 KJV

Lord,

I can remember when I thought my strength was my own. I can remember when I thought I had everything I needed to make it in life—without You. In some ways, that memory is not so far in the past. But I thank You today that I know how wrong I was—I have no strength but in You.

The horse is a symbol of strength and power, but even the strength of a thousand horses could not give me the security and protection I find in Your presence. And my legs are not strong enough to take me over the mountains of obstacles that lie in my path each day. I depend on You, Lord. I trust in Your mercy.

I look back over my walk with You and see all the places where You taught me to depend on You. I have watched You make my life secure when everything around me seemed to be collapsing. I have felt Your sustaining grace when I had no human strength left to face life. So today, and for the rest of my days on earth, I will put my only hope in Your love, for it has never failed.

Amen.

A cheerful heart is good medicine, but a crushed spirit dries up the bones.
PROVERBS 17:22

Dear Lord,

Thank You for the merry hearts—those people who are always ready with a song, a happy word, a little good humor. Thank You for their words of encouragement to soothe and mend the spirit. They are greatly loved and should be.

I can't help but wonder though about those whose hearts are not merry. Those individuals whose spirits have been broken. Those individuals who have suffered such hurt that they have become hard and negative. Crushed by the circumstances of this world, their bones have literally become dry and hardened. I see them every day, Lord—people like the waitress who served us lunch the other day or the teenager who shouted obscenities at a passing driver or the angry mother screaming at her children in the supermarket.

Lord, I pray that by the power of Your Holy Spirit, You would give me a merry heart. Heal my own hurts and make me whole so I can bring joy and sunshine to those who so desperately need it. Then give me the opportunity to act as a balm for those I encounter whose spirits have been crushed. Give me kind and encouraging words to speak and a heart full of love. Help me to be Your messenger of hope and healing.

Amen.

Whatever your hand finds to do, do it with all your might.
ECCLESIASTES 9:10

Dear Lord,

Behold my day.

Four bowls of cereal. Toothbrush patrol. Diaper changes. Zippers, buttons, and shoelaces. Packs, coats, mittens, and lunches for the school kids. Dress the baby. Sweep up the cereal. Scrub toilets. Diaper changes. Three loads of laundry. Vacuum. Pick up toys in the family rooms, kids' rooms, kitchen, living room. Candyland. Barney. Diaper changes. Make the beds. Water the plants. Make lunch. Clean up. Phewww! I take a coffee break. I pay for the coffee break when I discover my new red lipstick ground into the carpet. Thirty minutes with the carpet shampooer, but the stain still shows. Diaper changes. Naps. Another load of laundry. Dusting. Schedule appointments with the pediatrician, dentist, and portrait studio.

The babies are up. More diaper changes. Older kids arrive home from school. Snacks. Clean up. Homework. Barney—again. Start dinner. Set table. Answer a half-dozen requests from my precious black holes of need. Husband home. Dinner. Baths. Pajamas. Bedtime. Dishes. Fold the three loads of laundry piled on the sofa. Drinks of water.

Lord, remind me often that scrubbing toilets and sweeping up cereal is part of a sacred mission to love and care for my family, to provide for their needs, to make them feel secure and loved. Help me do what You have given me to do with all my might.

Amen.

The winter is past; the rains are over and gone.
Flowers appear on the earth; the season of singing has come.
SONG OF SOLOMON 2:11,12

Loving Father,

Thank You for sending the springtime. When the ice has crusted the earth too long, I feel desolate in spirit and in need of Your warmth. Now that the snow is melting into tiny rivers, cleansing the barren earth, I feel my inner spirit come alive once more.

On a beautiful spring day, I can see You all around me. Your deep desire to nurture blesses the withered flowers with new life. This sign of Your love gives me hope in my struggle to grow in spirit. As the budding earth flourishes, so my soul opens to Your touch, and I am renewed.

Your seasons give me a better understanding of who I am. Surely I was born to springtime, a tiny bud sprouting from Your love. Then as summer approached, my youthful bloom grew magnificent. In the autumn of life, I felt a quiet peace that I never noticed in my youth, and my colorful bloom deepened in hue. I suspect the snow will come one day, in the "winter of my soul," and the wind will carry my blossoms to another shore. But I will discover the lilting song of a bluebird and yellow daffodils, for You will be there to take my hand and lead me to the warmth of Your eternal spring.

Amen.

In repentance and rest is your salvation,
in quietness and trust is your strength.
ISAIAH 30:15

Oh Father,

How foolish I have been! I have wanted peace, quiet, and rest. I have searched for them, longed for them, and yet all the while You stood by offering them to me. I could have come to You long ago, repented, and found true peace. You would have sheltered me in Your arms and restored my strength. You would have been a haven to me, a safe harbor, my resting place.

Forgive me for the times when I have turned away like a two-year-old who wants to "do it myself" even when he isn't able. I wanted to say, "I'm strong. I'm capable, and I can do it." In pride I turned my back on Your offer. Thank You that in Your love, You waited.

Now, Father, like the prodigal son I ask for Your help. Oh, how I need You! I don't want to be a stiff-necked, stubborn child. Teach me to trust in You. Thank You that You did not turn Your back on me but patiently waited. You are a gracious Savior and full of mercy. Teach me to wait for You, for Your guidance, and for Your support. Purify my heart and cleanse me. Thank You, Lord, that I can call out to You and You will answer me. Thank You for Your goodness toward me.

Amen.

"For I know the plans I have for you," declares the LORD,
"plans to prosper you
and not to harm you, plans to give you a hope and a future."
JEREMIAH 29:11

Everlasting Father,

It's such a relief to know that I don't have to worry about the future because You have big plans for me. You know every detail of my life—who I am, what I will do, and what I will become. Before I was even born, You knew my name and my destiny. It is hard for me to comprehend such a thing. I struggle to find potential within myself, yet You have carefully set in place wonderful things for me!

Forgive me, Lord, for the times I have doubted whether my prayers would become a reality. For You have brought me to this point, and I can clearly see Your gentle hand at work orchestrating my steps. Though I still wonder what lies ahead, I will remember that You are faithful and Your timing is perfect.

Lord, I believe Your promise that You have a marvelous plan for my life—a plan that is more than I could ever imagine possible. My hope and my future are found only in You. I pray that You alone will order my steps and that my steps will lead me to the center of Your perfect will.

Amen.

The LORD *is good to those whose hope is in him,*
to the one who seeks him;
it is good to wait quietly for the salvation of the LORD.
LAMENTATIONS 3:25,26

Lord,

For a long time I was afraid to seek You too diligently. What if You were to call me to a desolate foreign land? I could never survive without my computer, my cell phone, my double stroller, and my whole milk latte. These "things" are the bedrock of my existence.

And the "waiting quietly" part, Lord—I have a hard time doing that, even when I'm waiting for a waitress to bring my order. If patience is a virtue, You and I both know I'm in big trouble.

The good thing is that You already know all of this. You know my weaknesses better than I do. This is my only hope. Of course I know that You would never send me anywhere without giving me the strength, the resources, and the courage to do what You have asked me to do. Strengthen my faith to the point where I won't be so pathetically grasping for my comfortable life; but instead, I will have the courage to face whatever life lessons You have for me to learn. And, Father, could I please have my whole milk latte one more day? Just kidding, Lord.

Amen.

I will put my Spirit in you and move you to
follow my decrees
and be careful to keep my laws.
EZEKIEL 36:27

Lord God,

The deepest desire of my heart is to obey all Your laws and decrees. But in my own human strength I will fail, for many times I am too confused to see what is right. What a refreshing thought, Lord, to know that You will help me!

Every day I hear noisy voices competing for my attention. Many of them are trying to entice me to follow different beliefs. They are loud and convincing, but I can feel Your Spirit within me warning me that something isn't right. Help me see through false claims and recognize those ideas that would lead me away from You.

How comforting it is to know that Your Spirit lives in me and that You will always be with me to help me in the confusing times. I know You will always move me to follow the right path—Your path. I live and move and have my being in You. I will not fear that the loud, confusing voices will ever lead me away from following Your righteous law, because Your Spirit will always show me the way. Thank You, oh Lord, for being such a loving and protecting Father.

Amen.

He is the living God and he endures forever;
his kingdom will not be destroyed.
DANIEL 6:26

Eternal God,

You are the compassionate Lord Who parts the waters and draws Your people to You. Many storms have risen against Your kingdom in an effort to separate Your people from You and overthrow Your throne, but You are the living God Who endures forever.

No angel or human being crowned You King of kings and Lord of lords. Your kingdom sits on a plateau that angels cannot reach. It sits far above the heavens. The galaxy is merely the basement of Heaven and this planet just a speck of dust. We are nothing in comparison to You. Our greatness comes only from Your love for us. That love surpasses all human knowledge and understanding. It is a jewel amid dull rocks—a morning breeze ushering in a new day. Your love completes us in everything we once lacked. You sit at the pinnacle, Your love and power immutable to the hateful ways of the wicked.

Thank You, Lord, for looking down from Heaven and having pity on me. Thank You for pouring out Your love on me and answering my cry for help. Thank You for loving me before it was ever possible for me to love You in return. Thank You, Lord, for Your great mercy! I will forever give You praise!

Amen.

You must return to your God; maintain love and justice, and wait for your God always.
HOSEA 12:6

Lord of Limitless Love,

You continually call Your people back to You. That implies that we have left You—countless times, if I read the Bible correctly. That makes me uncomfortable. Oh, I can see where others are fickle and unfaithful, but I'm not used to thinking of myself in that way. After all, I am a faithful husband, a good father, a loyal church member, and . . .

Still, I have to admit that my focus does tend to wander away from You and Your will. I let myself be seduced by the lure of material comfort and the little luxuries that only make me lazy and drain my bank account. I make excuses for ignoring the plight of the poor. Yeah, You're right, Lord, I do need to return to You—again.

Again. That word is what makes Your love so amazing. You never give up on me; You call me back to Yourself again and again. Then You patiently wait for me to come to my senses, return to You, and correct my priorities. I am humbled by Your love and patience. Help me accept Your forgiveness and love, but keep me from taking You for granted. I love You, and I truly am grateful for Your grace.

Amen.

I will pour out my Spirit on all people.
Your sons and daughters will prophesy, your old men will dream dreams,
your young men will see visions.
JOEL 2:28

Dear Father,

You are perfect in all Your ways. You have no equal, no balance. You are not a boastful God, even though You have every right to be. You are Lord of the gentle, the merciful, the pure, the hungry, the poor, and the martyrs. In a field of daisies, You are Lord of the dandelions. Your Spirit touches all of us, carrying Your Word as seed throughout the countryside.

I dream of a day when I will look out across this land and see fields spilling over with dandelions. Your thoughts will be our thoughts, and we will surrender them to the wind of Your Spirit. Through You, we will see our dreams, our visions, come to pass. I worship You with all my being. I celebrate, because if You had not sent Your Spirit, there would be no wind. We would only be scattered dandelions cowering in the shadows of daisies.

Thank You for the wind of the Holy Spirit that carries the precious seed. Thank You for allowing me, through Your Holy Spirit, to partake of Your greatness. Thank You, Lord, for letting me play a part in Your kingdom.

Amen.

Let justice roll on like a river, righteousness like a never-failing stream!
AMOS 5:24

Eternal Lord,

In a world where justice often seems to be no better than a glorified auction, I am so thankful that Your justice is not for sale. It doesn't matter how much money I have or whether I'm famous or if I have any influential friends. None of that matters. The only thing that is important is what's in my heart. As long as I have You there, justice can be mine.

In a world where righteousness is regarded by many as an inconvenient concept that no longer applies, I am so thankful that Your righteousness is unending. It doesn't matter how many times I've sinned or when I've been too busy to ask for forgiveness or to whom I could have witnessed but didn't. None of that matters. The only thing that is important is what's in my heart. As long as I have You there, righteousness can be mine.

Lord, You offer so much to those who will welcome You into their hearts. Like unstoppable forces of nature, I pray that both Your justice and Your righteousness will continue to gain strength. Let no barrier contain them as they transform each and every life in their path. And I pray that, along the way, they will sweep me up and carry me closer to the boundless ocean of Your love.

Amen.

The day of the LORD *is near for all nations.*
As you have done, it will be done to you;
your deeds will return upon your own head.
OBADIAH 15

Righteous Lord,

How gracious You are to all those who call on Your name. How merciful You are to all those who place their trust in You. Reach out Your hand one more time to those who have not yet responded to Your love and forgiveness. Touch and soften their hearts. Give them the great gift of repentance. For I know, Father, that You would have every man, woman, and child come to know You and be with You forever in Your kingdom.

Father, I ask You also to forgive me when I fail You. Speak sternly to me when I am considering an unrighteous path. Help me to judge my own heart so that I can always stand confidently before You. Give me the courage and wisdom to obey all Your commands. For when I see You face to face, I wish to be pleasing in Your sight.

I know that one day You will judge the world, righteous Father. The people from all nations will fall on their knees before You. On that great day, it is my prayer that I may be found worthy to stand in their midst and proclaim Your name with all the saints.

Amen.

I will praise and thank you while I give sacrifices to you, and I will keep my promises to you. Salvation comes from the LORD!

JONAH 2:9 NCV

Oh Loving Father!

You are marvelous! You delivered Jonah from his disobedience and set him on a path of submission. You broke his heart of stone and mended it with the oil of gladness. Truly, salvation comes from Your hand!

I lay my life before You, Father. With Jonah, I declare my intent to keep my promises to You. I know I am weak. I know I wander from Your path in many ways. I seek my own will, my own resolution to problems. I struggle with complete surrender to You, Lord. Grant me a heart free from the prejudices of life that limit my faithfulness to You. May my life be an offering—a willing, living sacrifice that seeks Your direction and goals above all else.

Let me echo Jonah's words of praise and thanksgiving for all that You are, for all that You do. May I find Your hand in all that encompasses me and lift my heart in grateful praise, regardless of my circumstances or surroundings. May my lips resound with words of blessing and glory and honor for Your mighty salvation. You alone are worthy, Lord, to receive the acclamation of my soul. Keep me centered in You. Focused on You. Faithful to You. Always.

Amen.

As for me, I watch in hope for the LORD, I wait for God my Savior; my God will hear me.
MICAH 7:7

My Gentle Shepherd,

I remember pressing my nose firmly against the cool windowpane, my quiet breath making clouds on the glass as I strained to hear the purr of Daddy's car pulling into the driveway. Then there was the morning I stood in the doorway of Grandpa's barn, alert even to the steady beating of my own heart, as I waited for the sun to burst over the horizon.

It was easy back then to be still and focus only on what I was expecting. Not so now! I'm so easily distracted by the hustle of everyday life. Lord, renew in me the excitement of anticipating Your involvement in my life. Teach me the joy of knowing You intimately as I block out the world's clamor to focus on Your still, small voice.

Sometimes I long for a thundering answer to my questions. With so much to be done, why would You want me to slow down to listen? Yet in this moment, as I kneel here by my bed, my energies exhausted, You cradle me in moonlight and I revel in the rhythm of Your heartbeat that drowns out all other sounds. I am eternally grateful that You choose to reveal Your heart to me in whispers and to enter my spirit on tiptoe.

Amen.

Look, there on the mountains, the feet of one who brings good news,
who proclaims peace!
NAHUM 1:15

Oh God,

You bring me peace—the "shalom" kind of peace that is more than just an absence of conflict or noise. Your peace brings health and wholeness to all areas of life. Therefore:

When my heart is anxious with the cares of earning a living, I will rest assured that You know my needs and will provide for me.

When my will is frustrated and my life feels out of control and at the mercy of others' whims, I will relax, knowing that I can place my trust in You.

When my past threatens to take captive my dreams for the future, I will remember that long ago You set me free to serve You in joy.

When my ideals and values are about to be overwhelmed by the wickedness and brutality in the world, I will welcome the good news that You have defeated these evils.

I ask Your blessing on those who proclaim and practice peace in hostile and lonely places: workers in shelters for victims of domestic abuse, agri-missionaries who teach poor farmers how to grow profitable crops in barren earth, mediators and diplomats who try to ease ethnic and national hostilities, teachers and counselors who work with children and teenagers.

Thank You, Lord, for granting Your peace. Grant me the courage to proclaim peace in my world.

Amen.

The earth will be filled with the knowledge of the glory of the LORD,
as the waters cover the sea.
HABAKKUK 2:14

Lord of all,

I praise You. Your name is so majestic. Your Word declares all that You are. Throughout time, man has trusted in other gods, but I will trust in You. There is so much to learn about You because You are so vast. When I look at the depths of the sea, I understand how powerful You are. When I look up to the sky above, I see the richness of Your presence. Lord, when I come to You with my heart, I understand the unfolding of Your love.

Teach me Your ways, that I may tell others about You. Everywhere I look, I see what You have created with such power and patience. Lord, You keep the mountains from crumbling into the sea while at the same time holding a sparrow contentedly in Your hand. You are in every cloud and every breeze. I praise You for all this and more. Let Your glory shine through me.

I place my life within Your hands, Lord. Let Your will be done through me. My heart's cry is to proclaim Your glorious works through all I do. Glory to You; I praise You, Lord of all!

Amen.

The LORD *your God is with you, he is mighty to save.*
He will take great delight in you,
he will quiet you with his love, he will rejoice over you with singing.
ZEPHANIAH 3:17

Father God,

How amazing and comforting it is to know that You delight in me. I can't always understand why You love me with all of my faults and issues, but You do. Like a father who delights in the antics and joys of his small children, You love to watch me grow and learn; and You rejoice in even my smallest successes.

This is particularly wondrous because apart from You, I am nothing and have nothing to give. You are the very Source of my life. Without Your constant presence in my life, I would experience only chaos and confusion. Yet there is nothing I will encounter that is too big for You, if only I remember You are with me.

When I face challenges and difficulties today, may I remember to seek You. Let me find peace and rest in You, knowing that You are mighty to conquer even my biggest mountains. May I learn to be quiet in Your presence so that I can hear Your special words for me. What beautiful songs of love You must pour out over Your children! I will always remember to give You thanks for the blessings You sing over my life.

Amen.

My Spirit remains among you. Do not fear.
HAGGAI 2:5

God of Power and Might,

Whatever my situation, I will not fear because I know Your Spirit remains with me, as You have said again and again in Your Word.

Because of Your promise to Abraham, I will not be afraid. You are my shield, my very great reward. Because of Your words to the children of Israel through Moses, I will not be afraid, but I will stand firm and see the deliverance You will bring me today. Because of Your promise to Joshua, I will be strong and courageous; I will not be terrified or discouraged, for You will be with me wherever I go. Because You spoke to King Jehoshaphat, I will not fear because the battle is not mine, but Yours. Like David, even though I walk through the valley of the shadow of death, I will fear no evil, for You are with me.

As You told Isaiah, You are the Lord, my God, Who takes hold of my right hand. You told Your people through Jeremiah, "Do not lose heart or be afraid when rumors are heard in the land . . . rumors of violence," (Jeremiah 51:46) so I, too, will keep heart. As You have told me through Your Son, Jesus Christ, I will not let my heart be troubled or be afraid, for Your Spirit is with me always.

Amen.

This is what the LORD *Almighty says:*
"Administer true justice; show mercy and compassion to one another."
ZECHARIAH 7:9

Dear God,

Justice has become nearly impossible to find, much less to administer. We have distorted it to mean whatever seems right in each man's own eyes. We want our way rather than Your way. Truth and justice have become relative terms, Your righteous standard scuttled for a "feel-good" form of justice based on inflated conceit and selfish desire.

Oh Lord, how we need Your forgiveness. We have refused to listen to You, and sin has hardened our hearts. Your commandment to be merciful and kind to one another has been pushed to the side in our efforts to be first, to be self-satisfied, and to be empowered at all costs.

I ask You, Father, by Your persistent Holy Spirit, to soften our steely, disobedient hearts. Help us to unstop our ears and hear Your truth; only then can we become a discerning and just people and realize afresh Your perfect purposes for us. Reshape us, Lord, into the image of Your Son, Jesus, Whose mercy and compassion literally flowed from His hands, feet, and side on the cross. How we need You to keep wooing and turning us, reclaiming us as Your people. Please, gracious Father, don't ever give up!

Amen.

Bring ye all the tithes into the storehouse, that there may be meat in mine house, and prove me now herewith, saith the LORD *of hosts, if I will not open you the windows of heaven, and pour you out a blessing, that there shall not be room enough to receive it.*

MALACHI 3:10 KJV

Oh Lord,

You look on me when I am working. You watch me when I am playing. You know when I am thoughtful, and You listen when I am praying.

Therefore, oh God, I take comfort in knowing that You are with me when I am staring at a huge pile of bills. Bills for food. Bills for the house. Bills for all the things my family needs to live healthy and productive lives. You have promised to provide all we need—if I will seek first Your kingdom and its righteousness.

But I have to admit, seeking Your kingdom and living in Your righteousness get a little blurry when I look at the stack of bills before me. This month, as I sort them and list the payments due, I will include the item "tithe." Clear my vision, Lord, as I write the check and anticipate the part of the worship service when I will place my offering in the plate. I will listen for Your Spirit to say, "Well done, good and faithful servant," and I will rest securely in Your faithful promise.

Amen.

Love your enemies and pray for those who persecute you.
MATTHEW 5:44

My Loving Lord,

I'll be the first to admit that I am far from perfect. Though I was created in Your image, I am, after all, only human. I know I have developed quite a few imperfections over the years, and from time to time, I know these imperfections have created some enemies.

I also know that it is very difficult for me to turn the other cheek. When people hurt me, my natural inclination is to try to hurt them back. I guess it's just human nature, but that's only a small comfort when I feel my throat tightening and my fists clenching. When I stop to think about it, I know that the desire for revenge is very unhealthy. Aside from what it might cause me to say or do to someone else, seeking vengeance against my enemies is extremely destructive to me. It fills my heart with hatred and my spirit with spite.

Lord, help me see the goodness in those who hurt me. Fill my heart with forgiveness for past attacks. Grant me the patience and the self-restraint not to strike back at future wrongs. And never let me lose sight of the fact that my enemies are just as human, and therefore just as much in need of love and forgiveness, as I am.

Amen.

Even the Son of Man did not come to be served, but to serve, and to give his life as a ransom for many.
MARK 10:45

Heavenly Father,

Help me remember that my role is that of a servant, not a judge or a ruler. How many times do I allow pride or self-righteousness to deceive me into thinking that I have been called to set others straight rather than to set them free? Keep me, Lord, from a proud look and a haughty spirit. Teach me to humble myself under Your mighty hand, that You may exalt me in due time.

Oh God, may I never become so engrossed in my own interests and concerns that I fail to first seek You and Your righteousness. Help me to run with patience the race that is set before me.

Help me to keep ever before me the image of Your Son Jesus Christ Who, though He was a king, was willing to set aside His royal robes and to clothe Himself in the humble garb of a servant. Help me to remember how He came to this earth not to be ministered to but to minister, to give up His life so others could live.

May His faithful servanthood be a constant reminder of what You have called me to do and to be in His name and in His place.

Amen.

Whoever can be trusted with very little can also be trusted with much,
and whoever is dishonest with very little will also be dishonest with much.
LUKE 16:10

Lord,

I watched a father and daughter at the lake today. The father kept urging the child to come into the water, assuring her that it was not cold and he would be there to hold her hand. Finally the little girl tentatively reached out a trembling hand that was grasped by a firm, solid one, and the two explored the water with their toes and knees, giggling and splashing. The child's hesitant trust was replaced with an unwavering confidence and infectious enthusiasm. She gave her father a small bud of trust and it blossomed into a flower of laughter, fun, and joyous abandon.

Too often, Lord, I forget that only honesty will produce the confidence, trust, and dependability that is so necessary in relationships. Insincere promises, lapses of integrity, and "little white lies" will only breed doubt, deceit, and faithlessness in my relationships with others. Yet remaining faithful to my promises, sincerely saying what I mean, and following through on the tasks You have set before me, Lord, will solidify my relationships.

Help me today to be trustworthy in the little things and trust You, Lord, to work out the rest, holding Your hand in joyous abandon as we walk knee-deep through life together.

Amen.

No one has greater love than this, to lay down one's life for one's friends.
JOHN 15:13 NAB

Loving God,

People are like currents of surging water flowing downstream, parallel to each other, but often with interchangeable paths. You've given us all the same creek bed through which to course, but at times our streams become clogged with debris and the tributaries cease to flow. It's during these times that You teach us our most meaningful lessons.

When my course is hindered, I am helped in my vulnerability and learn to be gracious in my humility. And when my stream remains clear of rubble, I become unselfish enough to jump the rocks and help another to clear the wreckage from their flowing branch. You prepare me each time You reach Your hand to steady me in my weaknesses. Can I do less for those who cry out for help?

All this I have learned from You, Lord. You have taught me to let Your love flow to others like the pure waters of life. You have given me the perfect model on which to fashion myself. As a devoted Father, You firmly, but gently, guide me through the troubled waters; and having experienced this kind of love, I, too, become a vessel with healing powers. Help me always reflect Your love so I can be Your instrument of healing to others.

Amen.

Believe in the LORD *Jesus, and you will be saved.*
ACTS 16:31

Dear Saving Lord,

You know I love a bargain! Nothing lights up my eyes like a sign announcing, "SALE." However, my mom always told me, "If it seems too good to be true, it probably is." Judging from my basement full of junk, this saying has merit. Perhaps that is why I find it almost impossible to believe that such an immense and priceless treasure—salvation—can be mine at so little cost to me. All that is required is belief in You? How can it be? Surely I must do something in exchange for this wonderful treasure.

Oh, but I get it! Yes, this offer really is too good to be true. It was no bargain; there were no discounts for You. This priceless treasure did demand a tremendous price, certainly one I never could have paid! Yet You loved me so much that You paid the price for me. You paid full fare for my salvation, then offered it to me as a free gift.

Thank You, Lord, for paying the price so that I can enjoy everlasting fellowship with You. Thank You, Lord, for loving all humanity so much that You made the ultimate sacrifice. You paid the highest price, then offered the gift to anyone—everyone—who simply accepts it and believes in You. Thank You, Lord!

Amen.

We know that in all things God works for the good of those who love him,
who have been called according to his purpose.
ROMANS 8:28

My Lord,

I know it's childish, but it seems so unfair that I have to suffer and endure tests and trials when You could so easily change everything in an instant. Why can't You just rescue me from every difficulty and uncomfortable situation? Why don't You just protect me from any encounter that would cause my faith to be tested?

I'm asking the question, Lord. But really I already know the answer. Your love for me cannot be questioned. You have saved me from the greatest of all suffering and given me eternal life with You! You are the perfect Father. Without tests and trials to overcome, I would miss the opportunity to grow, to watch You work in my life—changing me, teaching me, and ultimately giving me the opportunity to experience the joy of becoming victorious over those things that challenge me.

Father, I cling to Your promise that in all things, no matter how difficult they may seem, You are working for my good. You are my greatest champion and protector, and You will never allow me to suffer more than I can endure. Teach me to see my circumstances from Your perspective—always trusting that You are in control.

Amen.

Do you not know that your body is a temple
of the Holy Spirit,
who is in you, whom you have received from God?
You are not your own; you were bought at a price.
1 CORINTHIANS 6:19,20

Dear Lord,

There are days when I get so wrapped up in myself and my own dreams that I forget I am not my own. I'm Yours. Oh Father, teach me to relinquish all my puny, human dreaming into Your hands and allow You to enact Your astounding dreams for me. You know what is best for me better than I ever will. You bought me. You own me. You see all of me, even the parts to which I am blind.

Somehow I sense that only by releasing all of myself can I truly be a temple of Your Holy Spirit. Enable that release in me every day. Please, Lord, convict me on the days I start taking myself back piece by piece. At all times keep me aware of my level of dependence on You and my need of Your Spirit to continually fill me.

What an incredible honor to be a temple of Your Holy Spirit! I am so unworthy of Your attention. You are so amazingly holy. My Creator! My Lord! My Redeemer! Teach me to lose myself in You so decidedly that I have no desire for my own selfish dreams!

Amen.

If any man be in Christ, he is a new creature: old things are passed away;
behold, all things are become new.
2 CORINTHIANS 5:17 KJV

Dear Father,

Early in the morning, I come before You. Before the day has started, while everything is fresh. Before the first rays of sunrise blush across the sky. The day is new, Lord, but I feel so old. My stiffened hands can barely grip the coffee mug I'm holding.

Really it's no surprise, Lord. I am human, living in a body that is slowly returning to the dust from which You made it. The aches and pains, the trials and struggles are part of life. But part of me asks, "Didn't You say that anyone in Christ is a new creature?" And the answer comes to me, "Yes. Your spirit has been made new. Every morning is like the first time you believed in Me. The old ways of thinking are gone. In their place I have put a new spirit, a new joy, a new appreciation for the things of life other than the purely physical."

As I face another day, I know it is truly fresh because You are living in me—and in all Christians. In us, You restore all to its original newness. Through us, You call the world to Yourself. For all who will believe, You will change everything old into something new and glorious through Your Spirit.

Amen.

You, my brothers, were called to be free. But do not use your freedom to indulge the sinful nature; rather, serve one another in love.
GALATIANS 5:13

My Loving Father,

For years, I was a prisoner who could see no farther than the bars of my cage. My mind was filled with questions of what life could be like on the outside. I was locked away in a damp, dark cell until You opened the door. There was a blinding light and a voice calling me to step out. As I stepped though the door, You wrapped Your arms around me and held me while I wept. It was not by force or bargaining that I was set free—it was by love.

Thank You, my gracious Father, for Your abundant love. When I look back at my shackles, lying, gathering dust, I see the perfect example of love in the drops of divine blood speckled around the lock.

Show me, Lord, how to love as You have loved. Please help me give myself to others as You have given Yourself for me. I want to share in wiping away the tears of crying children. I want to teach the fatherless and cradle the neglected. Please open me, petal by fragile petal, so Your love can become in me, not just a flower, but a garden.

Amen.

It is by grace you have been saved, through faith—
and this not from yourselves, it is the gift of God—
not by works, so that no one can boast.
EPHESIANS 2:8,9

Lord,

You have given me much for which to be thankful: a good job, a strong marriage, terrific kids, and trustworthy friends. I have done precious little to earn these gifts, and I certainly don't deserve them. I want You to know how grateful I am for these blessings that bring joy and fulfillment to my life.

Even more wonderful, though, is the gift of Your life in me. This life gives depth and value to all the other gifts You have so graciously given. It is a constant reminder of Your love for me and the promise of a secure future.

Your powerful, strengthening, gracious life in me—what an unimaginable gift! It is as wonderful and unexpected as my first bicycle, shining red with gleaming chrome fenders and training wheels, and as extravagant as the tape deck my wife gave me when we were newlyweds and couldn't afford such a luxury. Your life in me is practical, too, like the table saw my family gave me a few years ago. It allows me to take delight in creating something useful and beautiful (sometimes) for someone else. Thank You, Lord, for the inexpressible gift of Your life in me.

Amen.

Do nothing out of selfish ambition or vain conceit, but in humility consider others better than yourselves.
PHILIPPIANS 2:3

Lord,

It is difficult to rid myself of selfish ambition and conceit in a world that teaches success is only attained by pushing oneself to the front of every line. Conceit is little more than believing lies about myself. Protect me from these unnecessary traps. They are poor substitutes for true confidence gained through meeting needs and fulfilling worthy purposes.

You teach another way, the way of humility. This is not a weak, self-punishing martyr complex, but rather, a reality check. Humility reminds me that no amount of assertiveness will substitute for seeing and meeting other people's needs. It enables me to see another person's need, because I see my own. Humility is the raw material of compassion and love.

Forgive my selfish ambition born out of unmet needs. Forgive the hurt I have caused when I have thoughtlessly pushed myself to the front of the line. Remind me that unless I am secure in You, treating others better is a twisted game of pretending to be humble while punishing myself. Nothing You did, from touching lepers to washing feet, was weak or self-abasing. Your humility came from a secured identity in Your Father. May I also receive such strength from You so that I am freed to offer myself to another, to consider another better, to grow Your heart in me.

Amen.

Let the peace of Christ rule in your hearts,
since as members of one body you were called to peace.
And be thankful.
COLOSSIANS 3:15

Lord,

He thought I was wrong, but I didn't mean it that way. She thought I was mean, but I only thought she was straying from the truth. Harsh, critical words tore down relationships in an instant that had taken months to build. The stinging accusations were not true. In my anger, I wondered, *What gives people the right to inflict their wrong-headed thoughts on another person?*

Yet as I sit here alone with You, I dare not cling to the pain the hurtful words have caused. I do not want to follow the path where they lead, for I fear they lead away from You. Instead I choose to remember how You were despised and abused by those who misunderstood Your purpose. And still, You could teach us in the book of Luke to love our enemies and pray for those who mistreat us.

So today, I pray for those whose words have hurt me. I pray for myself because my own words are sometimes the source of my pain. I pray that everything I say will be tempered with Your love. And I will wait upon You, Lord, until my heart is filled with Your peace.

Amen.

Make it your ambition to lead a quiet life, to mind your own business and to work with your hands.
1 THESSALONIANS 4:11

Almighty God and Father,

Thank You for allowing me to come to Your throne of grace today. As I begin this day, may I be mindful of Your presence and do only that which pleases You. You have directed Your children in the work You want to be accomplished and have given us the talents and strengths needed to complete the tasks set before us. Let us do our work in accordance with Your will—quietly and peacefully, showing others the love You desire us to have for one another. Please let my work today be pleasing to You, and I give all praise and glory to You for every accomplishment.

Lord, You have directed us to live quiet lives and to mind our own business. Let me be content to love and accept my fellow workers, neighbors, and friends, encouraging and supporting them so that they will see Your love shine into their lives. Through serene words and gentle actions, let me impart Your wisdom into their hearts. Help me to be a blessing wherever I go, and enable me to see a rich harvest of souls coming to know and trust in You.

Thank You for the work You have given me. Thank You for the privilege of serving You.

Amen.

The LORD *is faithful, and he will strengthen and protect you from the evil one.*
2 THESSALONIANS 3:3

Dear Father,

I don't know how I could make it through this life without Your faithful promises. They are gifts to me—treasures more precious than gold. They fortify and defend me when I am fighting fear and discouragement. They give me courage when the evil one lies to me and tells me all is lost. They keep me on the right path.

When I feel alone and scared, Lord, I am comforted by Your promise never to leave me nor forsake me. When I am faced with a decision, I am encouraged to know that You have promised to give me wisdom. When I am in need, I remember Your promise to provide whatever it takes for me to live a godly life. When I fail You, Lord, I depend on Your promise of forgiveness. When I feel worn out by this life, I take heart because You have promised to give me the strength I need to complete the course You have set before me.

Thank You, Lord, for giving me something solid, something tangible to hold on to. Thanks for giving me the way of escape before I even encounter the problem. Your promises are food and water to my soul. They bring me peace and calm in the midst of every storm.

Amen.

Godliness with contentment is great gain.
1 TIMOTHY 6:6

Dear God,

Sometimes when I observe Your people, I think what fickle creatures we are, what peculiar things we do. We can change our minds so easily, reversing ourselves on a whim. I can remember spending one January day indoors, curled up next to a warm, cozy fire. Then for no good reason, I decided I needed some fresh air, so I hopped up and rushed outside. The chilly winter wind sent me right back inside again.

We want to be close to other people, but we want our solitude at the same time. We like being challenged and busy, but daydream about long, luxurious naps. We like vacations, but it's work that makes us feel useful and productive. No matter what we have, we are always wanting something else.

Lord, I'm reassured to know that You've planned a balance for my life and that You are with me, regardless of where I am or what my circumstances might be. I'm so glad that You are eternal and Your mercies endure forever. You bring stability to my life because You never change, and You are not subject to whims of fancy. You are my rock and my safety net, and in You, I find contentment, no matter what is going on in my life.

Amen.

Do your best to present yourself to God as one approved, a workman who does not need to be ashamed and who correctly handles the word of truth.
2 TIMOTHY 2:15

Lord,

I want to be approved by You—every thought, every word, every action. But too often I find myself seeking the approval of other people, even though I know how fickle they can be. Their good will can disappear as quickly as rain in the desert. I dare not base my self-esteem on the way people judge me. I need a more reliable standard than that, Lord. I need You.

Help me avoid measuring my worth by the dollars in my bank account, the labels on my clothing, or my job title. These are superficial and temporary at best. I want to work for You, not for hollow status symbols.

I want to be a worker who pleases You—a true craftsman who takes pride in his work. As the writer labors to find just the right word or the woodworker smoothes and caresses the grain to get just the right finish, give me patience to do the job right. As the seamstress delights in the texture of the fabric and the farmer gets pleasure from rich soil between his fingers, give me continued joy and satisfaction in serving You.

Amen.

When the kindness and love of God our Savior appeared,
he saved us,
not because of righteous things we had done, but because
of his mercy.
TITUS 3:4,5

Savior God,

Thank You that in Your kindness and love You sent Your Son, Jesus, to die on the cross for me so I could be made righteous in Him. Thank You for saving me, Lord, not because of the righteous things I have done, but because of Your mercy and grace. I can't even understand such infinite kindness, such selfless love. I can't comprehend it, but help me receive and share it with the people in my life.

Thank You for generously pouring out Your Holy Spirit, Who lives within me to strengthen and empower me. Now that I am justified by Your grace and have the hope of everlasting life, help me to be careful to devote myself to doing what is good, those things that are excellent and profitable.

Thank You, Lord, for calling me to be a channel of Your blessings. Help me live in such a way that others may see my good works and come to know that You are the Way, the Truth, and the Life. Help me walk in Your ways. May all that I say and do serve to show Your great love and kindness, for which I give You thanks and praise.

Amen.

Your love has given me great joy and encouragement.
PHILEMON 7

Dear Father God,

At the start of every day, Your love and mercy are renewed. Hallelujah! Praise You, Father, for the joy this brings to my heart! I truly believe that no harm can befall me, that I need fear no man. My life is guarded by Your Word, and I am protected by Your angels. If I stumble on my own, I know that You will pick me up and carry me.

What a blessing it is to love You. There is no peace like that of trusting in You for all of the answers I need. I can bring any question to You, no matter how insignificant. As I learn to trust You more, I realize that You are ever present. You have promised Your guidance if I seek to please You, and You always deliver what You promise. You never fail me or forsake me, and this gives me more comfort than anything this earth could offer. I am at peace knowing that You are in charge of my life.

No man or event can take my joy from me, for it comes from You. I can truly say that the world doesn't give me joy—and the world can't take it away.

Amen.

Let us hold unswervingly to the hope we profess, for he who promised is faithful.
HEBREWS 10:23

Faithful Father,

Forgive me when I follow crooked lines and unnecessary detours. Forgive me when I play hide-and-seek with hope, treating it as an uncertain commodity when life is confusing and unpredictable. Help me understand that the hope I profess is as strong and sure as You. When I doubt that hope, I am really doubting You.

You are the faithful promise-keeper. I know that, and yet so often I place more hope in the promise than in the One Who promises. Then it is easy to entertain doubts, to stack evidence in the wrong way. Then I am the one who swerves in faithfulness. I am the one who allows faulty information to steal my hope and leave me faithless.

Help me see Your faithfulness across the ages, all the way to me. May I understand how pointed, how personal, and how powerful Your faithfulness has always been. May I never substitute faith in circumstances, which will disappoint and fail me. You must be my first defense against doubt and faithless living. I set my sights on You, as promise-keeper, and commit my life toward the hope You call me to profess. Help me confidently profess that faithfulness as I see Your mercy anew.

Amen.

Who is wise and understanding among you? Let him show it by his good life,
by deeds done in the humility that comes from wisdom.
JAMES 3:13

Dear Father,

As I meditate on this verse, I see that the truly wise must be humble. For the closer we get to You, the more wisdom You impart, and the more wisdom You impart, the more we realize our own foolishness and lack of understanding.

Let me live humbly before You, Lord. Remind me that human wisdom is nothing to You, that the things that impress me are just passing shadows, wisps of transparent fragments that vaporize to nothing. It doesn't matter how many diplomas hang on my wall or what Ivy League school is my alma mater. You alone are the source of true wisdom, and if I don't know You and Your ways, I know nothing. And if I know nothing, I can do nothing worthwhile.

Let me know You. Show me Your ways. Let me give my life and share my blessings. Give me the eyes to see the hurts and attend to the sad or discouraged. Give me the strength to meet the needs of the poor and yet tend to my own responsibilities. Let me have compassion and words to inspire. Let my deeds be good in Your eyes. Give me wisdom to see what truly matters.

Amen.

Above all, love each other deeply, because love covers over a multitude of sins.
1 PETER 4:8

Dear Lord,

He makes me so angry! How could he embarrass me in front of my friends? This time he's gone too far. Just wait. I'll get even.

Oh, Lord, I'm not in the mood to hear that I should love more, love deeper. I want to hug my anger close for just a bit longer. Must You remind me of Your perfect love which loves a most unlovable me? Won't You allow me to savor my thoughts of retaliation a bit before You shift my Christian conscience into overdrive? Yes, I know what You call me to do. But human nature seems to demand that I get even when I am wronged. To look past the insult takes more love than I can muster on my own.

Okay, Lord, Your love wins again. I'm ready to release my anger to You. Fill me with more of You. Just as a fresh blanket of snow hides the earth's imperfections, cover afresh my multitude of sins with Your love. Might I be so filled with love and concern for others that I hardly even notice when I am wronged. Thank You for loving me with such a supernatural love. Now may I respond to that love by letting it shine through me to others!

Amen.

The LORD *is not slow in keeping his promise, as some understand slowness. He is patient with you, not wanting anyone to perish, but everyone to come to repentance.*
2 PETER 3:9

Lord,

You are the original promise-keeper. Time after time You have done what You said You would do. You kept Your promise to give a son to Abraham and Sarah. You empowered Moses to lead the Israelites to freedom, just as You promised him You would. You promised the prophets of old that You would send a redeemer to restore the human race to right relationship with You, and You fulfilled Your promise in a gloriously unexpected way through Your Son, Jesus.

Thank You for being so patient with us humans—for accepting us just the way we are. Your patience has meant salvation for me and countless others who have turned from their self-centeredness and focused their trust on You.

Now, Lord, I await Your promise to come again to the earth. Give me faith to trust in Your promise and wait expectantly for Your return. Even though more than nineteen hundred years have passed, I believe that You will keep Your promise just as You always have. And I pray for those who have no hope. Help me point them toward You, through my words and deeds.

Amen.

*How great is the love the Father has lavished on us,
that we should be called children of God!
And that is what we are!*
1 JOHN 3:1

My Loving Father,

What a privilege it is to be called Your child—to bear Your name! Yet it's a lot to live up to as well. My actions and attitudes reflect back on You. If I am truly Your offspring, my life should reveal Your characteristics and attributes.

As a teenager, I remember my parents saying, "Be good. Your actions, good or bad, reflect not only on you, but on your whole family, and on us as your parents as well." And Lord, how many times have I heard the comment, "Your son looks just like you!" Obviously, those making the observation don't know that we adopted our son as a toddler. Still, they are right. He does look just like us. He has subconsciously picked up our mannerisms and idiosyncrasies through shared family life. None of us can help but assume some of the characteristics of those with whom we spend our days.

Oh Lord, as each day goes by, may I resemble You more and more. May my life bring You honor and glory. May I always be aware that others are watching me to learn more about You. I want so much, Lord, to reflect positively on the family name.

Amen.

And this is love: that we walk in obedience to his commands. As you have heard from the beginning, his command is that you walk in love.

2 JOHN 6

Precious Father,

Today, I prepare to face a world that seems to ignore You. As I read this verse, I think about all the people I might encounter. Some of them will be good and decent. Others will be out of control. So many I meet seem to have no moral grounding to help them do what is right.

Even I, sometimes, chafe at the idea of obedience. That word has often been used in connection with harsh and forced compliance. But I hear Your Word say that obedience is love. Obeying Your commands is a two-way street of love. You loved me enough to give me a moral compass so I wouldn't lose my way. I love You, Lord. And I want to show You that I trust You by doing what You say. Though I can't see the immediate effect, I know that doing what is right is best in the long run.

Today, Lord, as I walk with You, please remind me of Your commands. Open my ears to hear Your voice; check me when I am tempted to do wrong. Help me walk with You this day in obedient love so others may see Your Spirit shining through me.

Amen.

Dear friend, do not imitate what is evil
but what is good.
3 JOHN 11

My Father,

I live in a world preoccupied with appearances. We seem to put more emphasis on how a person looks than who that person is. We make far-reaching value judgments often based on nothing more than what people say about themselves, and we sometimes pattern our own behaviors after those whose appearances we find appealing. But appearances can be deceiving, and it's easy to be fooled by an elegant face or an eloquent phrase.

Amidst all the hype and the hero worship, I sometimes lose sight of the fact that actions should speak louder than words. I have to remind myself that how people look or act in public is really not nearly as important as how they live their lives in private. It's uncommon to see people encourage others to do what is right, then immediately forget or just plain ignore their own good advice.

Father, I pray that You will grant me the wisdom to not be deceived by evil. Help me have the vision to see through its disguises and the strength to reject its persuasions. Father, help me remember that Your example is the one I most need to follow, and please help me imitate Your goodness without becoming an "imitation person."

Amen.

Be merciful to those who doubt.
JUDE 22

Dear Lord,

Sometimes I wonder if You wrote this verse just for me. I make doubting Thomas look perfectly resolute. I am questioning and skeptical by nature. I can't keep from doubting. What about this? What about that? Just when I think I've got it all figured out, You throw me something else to grapple with. Each bout with Your mysteries strengthens my faith in You.

Like Jesus on the cross, I sometimes feel that You have forsaken me. Where are You in the tragedies that mark our days? Where are You in what seems to be senseless suffering? Sometimes I can see Your hand right away. More often, it seems to take forever; and some things, I'm sure I'll never understand in this lifetime. That's such a bitter pill for me to swallow, Lord.

Help me accept that I cannot know everything now. You have given me a million reasons to trust You, and yet I'm always begging for more. Open my eyes to see Your miracles all around me, in the sunset, in the daisies, in my children. Open my ears to hear You speaking to me in the clamor of the day and the stillness of the night. Open my heart to receive more of Your love, the true evidence of Your presence in my life. And until then, Lord, be patient with me; I tend to be a doubter.

Amen.

Those whom I love I rebuke and discipline.
So be earnest, and repent.
REVELATION 3:19

Holy Father,

I surrender myself to You and lay myself at Your feet, guilty as charged. You are the great judge of heaven and earth. Pour out Your mercy on me, and cleanse me from all unrighteousness. Give me a heart that is clean and white, holy and pure, washed in the blood of Jesus, my Savior. And then, Lord, receive me as Your child.

Thank You, Father, for making a way for me and refusing to leave me in my sin, forever separated from You. Thank You for reaching out to me when I was weak and feeble and completely without strength. Thank You for Your love that draws me to repentance and gives me the courage to try again.

Father, I accept Your discipline in my life. I see it as the gift of a good Father—a Father Who will not allow His child to wander far from the fold. I pray that it will always be this way. Though Your discipline is often painful, I know that when I respond to it, I am opening up my life to receive Your grace and blessing. I know that it gives me the confidence to come into Your presence and ask You to meet my needs. Thank You, Father, for Your tender mercies.

Amen.

You intended to harm me, but God intended it for good to accomplish what is now being done, the saving of many lives.
GENESIS 50:20

Dear Lord,

I've always believed that You have a wonderful plan for my life and that You make all things work together for my good. But I never imagined that You would actually use the strategies of my enemies to carry out Your plan. You constantly amaze me!

As I read these words spoken by Joseph, I can only imagine how he must have felt when his own brothers threw him into a hole and told his father he was dead; then he was sold into slavery in Egypt and unjustly cast into prison. He must have felt alone, betrayed, forgotten, and humiliated, but somehow he never lost faith in You or Your plan for his life. And one day, he found himself standing before Pharaoh, the most powerful man in the world, and being raised to a position of prominence just in time to save his family from famine and starvation.

Lord, I want to have that kind of faith. I want to trust You so much that no matter what happens to me, I can be certain that You are at work turning the strategies of my enemies into great blessings for my life and the lives of those I love. I place my future into Your hands.

Amen.

And the LORD said unto Moses, I will do this thing also that thou hast spoken:
for thou hast found grace in my sight.
EXODUS 33:17 KJV

Dear Lord,

When You speak to me, I know I can trust in Your words because You always keep Your promises. How reassuring it is to know You are dependable in all things and You always do what You say You will do.

Believing Your promises and knowing Your faithfulness to me make it possible for me to be bold in my service to You. How blessed I am to have found favor in Your sight. Although I have a burning desire to serve You faithfully, I sometimes fall short. It is comforting to know You look beyond my faltering ways and see my heart. There are times when I feel like no one understands or is interested in my problems, but I know I can always bring them to You. For You will listen and help me remain strong in my spirit.

May I always remember that You suffered many things and understand how I feel. You will be with me in the midst of any trouble, illness, grief, or sorrow that may befall me. You have promised never to leave me nor forsake me, and I have placed my faith in those words. Thank You, Lord, for Your faithfulness.

Amen.

Among those who approach me I will show myself holy;
in the sight of all the people I will be honored.
LEVITICUS 10:3

Wonderful Lord,

Thank You for this reminder that You are to be honored above all things. You have created all things. You both set up and remove principalities and powers in Your timing and according to Your will. You know the number of gray hairs on my head, and You graciously provide for my every need, even when I'm not aware of it. You are worthy of my praise.

Yet even in Your awesome majesty, this verse reminds me that You are approachable, Lord. I will probably never sit down and talk with the President at the White House. I wouldn't be able to walk through the door of my state representative's office without an appointment made months in advance. I doubt I could even drop in to see my pastor unannounced and find him available for a chat. But I can come before You anytime, for any reason, and You will not turn me away. Lord, I am humbled. I stand in awe.

Today, I thank You for opening Your heart to hear my prayer. I rejoice in Your presence. I yield my life and my plans to Your will. Find me faithful in my praise, constant in my obedience, and unswerving in my allegiance and honor to You, oh Lord.

Amen.

Must I not speak what the LORD puts in my mouth?
NUMBERS 23:12

Gracious Lord,

Challenge me this day to be faithful to the calling You have placed upon me for this hour. Oh Lord, let the words of my mouth be fruitful, as a fountain releasing the rivers of Your life to all who thirst. Out of the reservoirs of Your fullness, let me speak of Your unending deliverance and of Your marvelous hope.

Except You speak out of Your heart through Your servants, what can be done in the earth? If I'm to serve You to the greatest extent, I must hear Your voice permeate the depths of my being. The very issues of Your love must spring forth out of the well You have filled deep within my soul.

Oh, should I not speak of Your goodness and the floods of joy it unfolds? Help me, Lord, to constantly proclaim Your promise to raise us up when we fall and give us strength to stand when we have been cast down. Though the heavens pass away and the mountains fall down before the people, they will not hear. Unless Your voice pricks their hearts and Your tender touch soothes and awakens their spirits, they will perish. Put Your words into my mouth, and I will shout them to those who need to hear.

Amen.

And now, O Israel, what does the LORD your God ask of you but to fear the LORD your God, to walk in all his ways, to love him, to serve the LORD your God with all your heart and with all your soul.
DEUTERONOMY 10:12

Oh Lord,

As I read Your words today, I hear the all-important question: "What does God ask His people to do?" The answer rings out loud and clear in four commands: fear, walk, love, and serve.

We do fear You, Lord. We have deep respect for Your mighty power. How could we not stand in awe of the only One Who creates and sustains everything that exists? Because we know You as a sovereign God, we happily walk in Your ways. The paths of the world lead us to destruction, but Your ways lead us to life.

Because we walk with You day after day, year after year, we have come to know the depths of Your love. We respond with love because You first loved us. It takes no stretch to imagine serving You, for we cannot really imagine serving any other. Our total being is wrapped up in reverencing You, walking in Your paths, and loving You. So the least we can do is serve You all the days of our lives. Thank You, God, for being so clear about what You want us to do.

Amen.

Choose for yourselves this day whom you will serve. . . .
But as for me and my household, we will serve the LORD.
JOSHUA 24:15

Dear Father God,

My life is full of choices and decisions. Between breakfast cereals and toothpaste options, it is a wonder my brain doesn't overload before I walk out the door every morning. And frankly, Lord, I hate making decisions!

There is one decision I know I must make on my own though. I can't pass it off to anyone else. That is the question of "Whom will I serve?" The choice is mine—all mine. Should I simply accept the god of the past, assuming if it was good enough for Grandma, it's good enough for me? Or will I take the easy way out, blindly following the crowd around me? The gods of self-gratification and material gain continually call out to me, too. Will I follow the lead of my peers and seek after these gods of the "good life"?

Oh Lord, I pray that You will protect me from such folly! Today, and every day, when opportunities arise to choose servanthood or selfishness, may I reconfirm my decision to follow and serve You. May I have the good sense to worship You—the One and only God above all gods and Lord of lords.

Amen.

Why do you ask my name? It is beyond understanding.
JUDGES 13:18

Oh God,

You are a God of many names but still one cohesive Being. I address You with one name, only to find my understanding so finite, so limited—and limiting. I name You Creator, but You are also Sustainer. I know that You are Father, but You are also Son and Spirit. I recognize You as compassionate Healer, but You are also righteous Judge.

Perhaps if I give You one name only, I can better understand and predict You. Yet if I can predict You, You are no longer God but a false image. There are no words that can hold all of Who You are. Words and names are merely openings through which I go to realize nothing can contain You—nothing.

Oh God, protect me from searching for names instead of searching for You. May I use Your names as merely the beginnings of the limitless person You are. Burst my small understandings. Explode my limited knowledge. May I find in You a completeness that needs no name. It is not a name that draws me to You. It is Your nature. I am speechless in the presence of the One I cannot name. Silent, I am finally ready to know You.

Amen.

Blessed is the Lord *who has not left you without a redeemer.*
Ruth 4:14 NAS

Dear Lord,

How Naomi must have rejoiced! How blessed Ruth must have felt! You gave them a child to carry on the family name. You provided for their needs as widows and relieved their struggle through the kindness and love of Boaz. You redeemed them, Your children, from the uncertainty of the present and gave them hope for the future.

And You, Almighty God, are still in the business of redemption. You opened Your heart and released Your only Son to death on a cross redeeming a fallen world to Yourself. You stretched out Your hand and poured blessing on Your people. You, Father, are the God of redemption. You are the God of grace. You are the God of love.

Blessed are You, oh Lord, for loving me. Find in my heart continual praise for Your compassion. Blessed are You, oh Lord, for paying the penalty for my sin. Find in my being remorse for my transgression. Blessed are You, oh Lord, for redeeming me from my sinful self. Find in my spirit acceptance of Your atonement. Blessed are You, oh gracious Lord, for all You have done. Find in my soul abandonment to Your will. I give You honor, glory, and praise as my Redeemer and King.

Amen.

Man looks at the outward appearance,
but the LORD looks at the heart.
1 SAMUEL 16:7

Oh Father,

How often I have valued another person by his outward appearance! I have foolishly thought that I could know the character of a man by looking at his face. I have judged people by their possessions, the kind of houses they live in, and even by the cars they drive.

You judge rightly, Lord, because You look at a person's heart. Teach me to judge with Your criteria. Teach me to value others, not by physical beauty or strength, but by inner character. What worth is outer charm if it covers malice or dishonesty? What use is health if inside a man's heart is degenerate? If his heart is pure before You, that is truly beautiful.

When You look at me, Father, and see my heart, be merciful. I pray that You will remember that I am dust and be gracious toward me. I know I can hide no sin from You. Every fault is laid open before You. You hear every unkind thought, and You detect every prideful stirring in me. Yet You still love me, Father. How good You are to me! Let the knowledge of Your perception of me lead me to repentance. Work on my heart; purify and soften it so it will be pleasing in Your sight.

Amen.

To the faithful you show yourself faithful, to the blameless you show yourself blameless, to the pure you show yourself pure, but to the crooked you show yourself shrewd.
2 SAMUEL 22:26,27

To the One Who Understands All My Ways,

When I was in sin and did not know the simplicity of Your love, You came to me as Savior. When I sought to know more of Your mysterious presence, You came to me as Teacher. Now that I know You as my friend and my salvation, You come to me as Father. Throughout the journey of my life, You have been all that I've needed—from Creator, to Physician, to Lord.

You are more infinite than the vast expanse of the heavens, and yet You show us the many facets of Your character and meet us where we are. In Your unfathomable wisdom, You show Yourself faithful to the faithful, blameless to the blameless, and pure to the pure. You approach those who practice evil with conviction—but also kindness.

Help me to be wise, faithful, blameless, and pure, that You will show Yourself in the same light. Help me to emulate Your character in all I do. Oh Lord, how I long to be more like You. How much I desire Your light to shine down into my life. Thank You for creating me in Your image to be called Your child.

Amen.

Give attention to your servant's prayer and his plea for mercy,
O LORD my God.
Hear the cry and the prayer that your servant is praying in your presence this day.
1 KINGS 8:28

Merciful God,

I come to You today with a humble heart. I am in need. I am in need of Your understanding and forgiveness. I am in need of Your mercy and grace. And I am in need of Your compassion and love.

I know I don't really deserve any of these things. In so many ways, I fall far short every day. I'm not always understanding with those around me, and I don't always forgive others the way I should. But I also realize that Your understanding and forgiveness are not reserved solely for those who "deserve" them. They are always free for the asking. You offer compassion and love to anyone who comes to You with an open heart. Please know that my heart is open wide today.

Lord, hear the urgency of my prayer. You alone know how hard I struggle to be the person You would have me be. You alone know how much I need the gifts only You can bestow. You alone know how desperately my heart yearns to be closer to You. And You alone can transform my life. I pray that You will indeed transform me, merciful God, that I might better serve You.

Amen.

Neither before nor after Josiah was there a king like him who turned to the LORD as he did—with all his heart and with all his soul and with all his strength,
in accordance with all the Law of Moses.
2 KINGS 23:25

My Heavenly Father,

I want always to love and serve You with all my heart and soul and strength. I want to stay on the path You have set for me.

Lord, You know that I don't intend to stray from Your path. It's just that I get preoccupied with what I want and where I want to go. Before I know it, I find that I have wandered away from You and Your perfect will for me. Lord, I need feet that refuse to leave the path. If only You could hedge me in and make me go Your way.

I know, though, that You have given me a free will, the power to choose my own path. Give me the resolve I need to choose Your way, Lord—not just some of the time but all of the time. I know that Your path is the way to the valley of blessing. It is the only way that offers hope and security. Your path is where my needs will be met. I surrender my will to Yours, Lord. Help me follow You with my heart and soul and strength and also with my feet.

Amen.

King David went in and sat before the L*ORD, and he said: "Who am I, O* L*ORD God, and what is my family, that you have brought me this far?"*
1 CHRONICLES 17:16

Father God,

Thank You for the joy that You bring into my life through my family. You have blessed us with immeasurable laughter, love, and comfort for the heartaches. I often feel as David must have felt when he spoke to You in amazement—Who are we that You have brought us "this far"?

I know that You have had Your hand on us. You've walked with us through the good times and the bad times. There have been some disappointments, Lord, but Your comfort and encouragement have always been there as well. You know, too, that my marriage has not been all I'd hoped or expected, but, I am beginning to realize that there are no perfectly happy and harmonious families out there. That's why I need to focus all my hopes and expectations on You.

When the times of disappointment come again, Lord, I will remember that You have brought us this far, and You won't desert us now. And also, Lord, for the times when my family and I seem to be strolling along in contentment, please remind us to rest in Your care and be grateful for the peaceful path. You have brought us this far, Lord. Thank You. Let's keep going.

Amen.

O LORD, God of our fathers, are you not the God who is in heaven?
You rule over all the kingdoms of the nations.
Power and might are in your hand, and no one can withstand you.

2 CHRONICLES 20:6

Mighty Father,

You know what I heard myself say today? "All we can do is pray." What a joke. Like prayer is some kind of feeble, last-ditch option when all the alternatives have failed. I know the truth, Lord. I know that prayer is the first and best option. The trouble is that my mind is so limited and my thinking so repressed that I still find it difficult to depend on something and Someone other than myself and my own efforts.

Forgive me for my arrogant independence. Help me always remember that prayer is more than feeble words tossed into the air. Prayer is nothing less than inviting the Creator and Ruler of the universe to come onto the scene and act on my behalf. It is stepping up to Your throne and asking that all Your limitless resources, both seen and unseen, be accessed to meet my need.

Thank You, Lord, for making me Your child and for defending me with all Your magnificent and unlimited power. From this day on, I will come quickly and enthusiastically into Your presence with my petitions. From this day on, I will put my trust in You, where it belongs.

Amen.

The gracious hand of our God is on everyone who looks to him,
but his great anger is against all who forsake him.
EZRA 8:22

Dear God,

It is a great comfort to know that Your hand is over me because I seek Your will daily for my life. You help me realize that I do not fight the battles of life alone, and although I may end up with scars, You will bring good into my life.

I remember that flat tire long ago. It was near midnight, and we were taking a detour. Our only flashlight wouldn't work, and there were no stars. We had to change the tire in total darkness, as we shivered in the cold wind. Giving thanks in all things was not easy at that moment. Then as we started on our way, we realized the bridge was out just a few feet down the road. There was nothing to warn us. The flat tire had saved our lives. Sitting there in the darkness just inches from possible death, we realized the "good" You bring into our lives.

Thank You, God, for loving me, for bringing good out of my circumstances. Give me the grace to pray for those who seem to deliberately scorn Your love. May I view the unfaithful through the eyes of faith.

Amen.

You are a forgiving God, gracious and compassionate, slow to anger and abounding in love.
NEHEMIAH 9:17

Gracious Father,

I humble myself and worship You with an open heart. No one can compare with You. Your grace and mercy have been extended to all through Your Son, Jesus. Your love reaches to the ends of the earth, to each and every person.

Father, I am thankful for Your Son. I know that because of His amazing sacrifice, I have an advocate in heaven. There is none Who forgives and heals like You. You are the greatest parent of all time. When You correct me, You love me. When You instruct me, You are compassionate toward me. Lord, You fill me with new hope and give me a vision of who I am becoming in You.

I stand before You as a child in need of Your comfort. Hold me close that I may feel Your love. The grace that You give sustains me. You are the best thing that ever happened to me because with You, I have hope in this life. I am not who I should be, but I will become that person because You are leading me—and walking with me—down the road. I can trust You, Lord, for You have shown Yourself faithful. Patient Savior, I am grateful for Your grace.

Amen.

No letter written in the king's name and sealed with his signet ring can be canceled.
ESTHER 8:8 NCV

My Lord God,

What power lay in the hands of a mortal king that his declaration would be set and unchangeable! Yet You, Lord, are more powerful than any earthly sovereign. You speak and kingdoms topple. By Your mouth authorities are established. Your words formed the very earth on which I walk, the water I drink, the plants and the animals that sustain my life.

Your words have promised me forgiveness for my sins and salvation through Jesus Christ. You have guaranteed me an eternity with You to worship and praise You forever. You have promised me wisdom and understanding, to quench my thirst for righteousness, to establish my faith, and to keep me from the evil one. You have declared Yourself to be my hope, my strength in time of trouble, my light in the darkness.

You have assured me that You will work everything for my good, that You will not let me be tempted beyond what I can stand, that You will provide for me and make me more like You. You have promised to be my comfort, my healer, my strength, my guide, and my peace. Sovereign King, Your words are stronger than those of any earthly king. They cannot be revoked. Turn my heart to Your words of assurance as I go throughout my day.

Amen.

Though he slay me, yet will I hope in him; I will surely defend my ways to his face.
Job 13:15

Father,

Like Job, I feel You have allowed me to be stripped of everything I ever held dear. In one breath, I want to say, "How could You!" In another, I want to say, "Please, God, deliver me! Please make this all a terrible dream!" Some days I feel as if I'm being spiritually crippled instead of being shaped into Your image. Will I even survive?

But in the midst of all my pain, I somehow hear a soft voice, a recurring thought, a message from You. Yes—You see my agony. You know my suffering. You hear my cries. And I feel You mourning the loss just as wretchedly as I mourn. You are my journey-mate. My rock. My healer.

Oh Lord, get me through this with a firmer grip on You than I've ever had. Help me be victorious and spiritually strong. Don't allow this tidal wave of tragedy to cripple me and rob me of my hope in You. Teach me to place my faith in You—not because of what You can do, what You promise, or Your ability to deliver me—but simply because You are God. And oh God, I dare to pray that You won't deliver me until I have learned all You want to teach me.

Amen.

O God, you are my God, earnestly I seek you;
my soul thirsts for you, my body longs for you.
PSALM 63:1

Lord,

You are the water of life. When the world seems like a spiritual Sahara, devoid of the values and beliefs that give color and texture to life, I trust You to keep me refreshed and growing. Without You, I would dry up and blow away.

So many people are already lost in the desert and don't even realize it. They think they are in paradise, with their money and houses, their parties and power trips, their pop psychology and self-made beliefs. But those things create false hope, like a mirage in the distance, and can't support life for very long. Help them see that their spiritual thirst can only be quenched by You.

Others know that they are lost in the desert but have given up hope of finding anything to quench their thirst. Perhaps they grew up in families where they never heard the truth. Maybe they have failed in their personal or professional lives and are tired of struggling. They could be abused or addicted. Whatever the reason, Lord, protect them from those who prey on the weak. Help me as I offer cups of cold water from Your fountain of life. May that taste give them hope and strength to take the next step toward You, the source of life.

Amen.

Those who sow in tears will reap with songs of joy.
PSALM 126:5

Oh Transforming Savior,

Tears turning to joy? Seeds of sorrow sprouting into harvests of happiness? I must confess that the logic of this verse eludes me. This seems like a topsy-turvy, mixed-up philosophy to me. Such a formula doesn't quite compute in my human way of thinking. But, Lord, as I reflect on Your Word today, a glimmer of understanding breaks through. Could it be that only those who suffer life's lowest lows can truly appreciate real joy when it comes along?

Come to think of it, the most joy-filled people I know are those whom I would consider the most unlikely. My friend has been battling with cancer, but it hasn't made her bitter. Rather, she finds each moment of life a precious gift from You. And the couple from my church, the proudest, happiest parents around, struggled for years with infertility issues, miscarriages, and stillbirths. When the day finally came for them to welcome their two adopted sons from Russia into their home, their joy overflowed.

In my humanness, I don't relish the idea of suffering. But, Lord, if in suffering I learn the art of a grateful spirit and a joyful heart, I make myself available to Your work in my life. Through good times—and bad—I am Yours.

Amen.

The lamp of the LORD *searches the spirit of man;*
it searches out his inmost being.
PROVERBS 20:27

Oh God,

Lately, I have felt You searching me—felt it in a painful way. You have been exposing my inmost being and showing me things about myself I'd really rather not see. In my human folly, I want to do the "Adam and Eve thing" and hide or try to pass the blame off on somebody else. But that has never worked with You. Relentlessly, You continue to shine Your light in the dark corners of my soul, asking me to relinquish every inch to You.

At last I've come to the end of myself, and I'm exhausted, tired of the struggle of wills between You and me. Finally, I'm going to say what I should have said weeks ago. Just take those corners of my soul and everything that's in them. Take them, God, and fill them with Your presence. Replenish me with the purity of Your love. Overwhelm me with Your precious presence.

And as I stand, spiritually naked before You, continue to shine Your lamp on me. But this time, oh Lord, let me feel the warmth of Your approval, rather than the heat of Your purging. Let me know that You have been pleased with my broken spirit, my contrite heart—sacrifices of my love and devotion for You.

Amen.

A man can do nothing better than to eat and drink and find satisfaction in his work.
This too, I see, is from the hand of God.
ECCLESIASTES 2:24

Precious Lord,

I really want to be a simple person—not simple in terms of being boring or unoriginal or foolish. I like to think I can be as exciting and creative and smart as the next person. But I do want to be spiritually simple. I want to know You in a basic, informal way, without letting life's distractions hinder our relationship.

I want to pursue spiritual wealth rather than material possessions. I want to have plenty to keep me busy but not let my job define me. I want my best friend's smile to be worth more to me than any amount of money. In a word, I want to keep it simple. After all, true happiness is an internal state that I can cultivate for myself, not an external possession that I have to buy in a store.

Lord, I pray that You will help me stay focused on what truly matters. Help me look inside myself, inside my heart, for the things I most need in my life. Don't let me get caught up in the pursuit of worldly goods. And let me live my life so people will know I am both simple and rich in Your Spirit.

Amen.

Many waters cannot quench love; rivers cannot wash it away. If one were to give all the wealth of his house for love, it would be utterly scorned.
SONG OF SONGS 8:7

Lord God,

Let love be my focus today. Help me love not only the lovable and those who love me, but those who are hateful, impatient, unfair, lazy at my expense, rude, unhelpful, resentful of my victories, and those who seem to take joy in celebrating my failures.

Help me love with Your supernatural love. Be patient with me when I fail. Forgive me when I'm tired and cranky and take it out on others. Thank You for letting me be honest. Thank You for letting me come to You with my anger, because You already know it exists. Thanks for the times that You've let me rant, the times You've listened to me beg You to "smite" the person who's harmed me. Thank You for letting me communicate these things to You, and thank You for teaching me how to love.

Most of all, thank You for loving me in all my moments of ungratefulness and generally bad behavior. Thank You for loving me when I haven't deserved it. Keep me reminded of that today, so I can recall what my love for others should look like.

Amen.

This is what the LORD says—your Redeemer, the Holy One of Israel: "I am the LORD your God, who teaches you what is best for you, who directs you in the way you should go."
ISAIAH 48:17

Dear Lord,

Maybe someday I'll find the humor in all this, but I'm not laughing right now! Since uprooting our family to a new home in a new city, it seems like I spend all my time driving around in circles, hopelessly lost.

My husband is frustrated, too. He ran out of gas this morning just two miles from home. When he called, I told him I would be there to rescue him in just a few minutes. But I hadn't taken into account the tangled web of unfamiliar streets. I'm sure I made every wrong turn possible in our small city. I frantically searched all points of the compass for the right road. The poor man wasn't smiling when I finally found him over an hour later. Neither was I.

Father, I feel overwhelming gratitude for Your guidance and direction in my life. I won't need to depend on my own limited resources to get "home." The map of my life is laid out before You. You know the way I should go, and You don't mind taking over the wheel. I gladly leave the driving and navigation of my life in Your hands. Guide me and direct me safely home, Lord.

Amen.

Call unto me, and I will answer thee, and shew thee great and mighty things, which thou knowest not.
JEREMIAH 33:3 KJV

Precious Father,

The image of You hovering over me with such unfathomable love both delights and saddens me. How patiently You stand waiting, Your arms overflowing with the abundance of gifts You want to shower upon me, Your child, an object of Your love and affection.

It shames me to think of how often I choose to stumble over and pick through the wreckage of this world, instead of coming to You, abiding where all of my needs are so perfectly met. How often have I filled my belly with bland, indiscriminate junk food, ignoring the rich feast You have spread before me . . . how eagerly You hold the chair for me.

I am foolish, Lord. Forgive me. My fumbling, hungering heart needs You—my only source of true fulfillment. Battered as I am by unwise and dissatisfying choices, I long to climb into Your lap, relax in Your accepting arms, and listen to Your soft words of forgiveness and the answers to my heart's deepest questions. Mete out to me, Lord, Your unsearchable truths. Instruct me in the way I should go. Make my heart ready for each new lesson. Create in me the longing to know You as well as I am known by You—this is my deepest desire, Father.

Amen.

Restore us to yourself, O LORD, that we may return.
LAMENTATIONS 5:21

Almighty Father,

As my adoration for You springs forth in surges of praise, from the deep recesses of my heart, my soul is consumed. I'm stirred from the core of my being with a fiery pursuit for that innermost fellowship reserved specifically for those who diligently seek You—that place where life itself loses its glow apart from Your manifest radiance warming the embers of my soul.

Let not the wandering thoughts within this carnal mind lead me astray, but let the chastisements of Your love and grace ever draw me to Your sweet haven of rest. Permeate, with Your mercies, the very air that envelops around me, that I may always yearn to return to Your glorious embrace.

Grant unto me, Lord, Your undeniable favor, that Your very heartbeat would echo within the chambers of my heart. Let those longings for Your presence cause me to return to the place You have created just for me. Except that You prepare the way, Lord, how can I return? Hover over me, and keep the pathway clear. Stir within me such a sense of Your care that I totally forsake any desire keeping me from a complete abandonment to You. Show me, Lord, and I will return. Touch me, Lord, and I will always remain.

Amen.

You will be my people, and I will be your God.
EZEKIEL 36:28

My God,

All my life I've wanted to belong to someone, to find a connection and a refuge of understanding, to have a best friend who knows my funny quirks—a true companion who will listen to my sorrows and joys. I've had friends who have come and gone throughout my life, but none who met this deep need for belonging. I understand now, that there's a place in my heart that can only be totally filled by You. All of my exquisite hopes and daring dreams find haven in Your sanctuary. You, Lord, are my dearest and most precious friend.

You are also the One in Whom I find my identity. I know from the book of Genesis that I was formed in Your likeness and created in Your image. How unique a design to show forth the splendor of God! I must be a precious possession to be formed from such an image. Because of Christ, Who became human, I literally bear Your stamp of approval, and my very existence is validated.

So much is demonstrated when You proclaim that we will be "Your people," and so much is approved when You declare, "I will be your God." It is an adulation to call You mine and an honor when You call me Yours.

Amen.

The LORD *our God is merciful and forgiving, even though we have rebelled against him.*
DANIEL 9:9

Lord God,

You are so faithful, so why is my heart so faithless? Even when I come before You in humility, like right now, I know I will be coming to You with this same beginning statement again and again. I seem to wander away at the slightest distraction. This is truly rebellion in me. So often I stand like a haughty and egocentric teenager before my loving and wise Father. Will I be grounded for the weekend? Will I lose my phone privileges?

No, unfortunately in my spiritual rebellion, the stakes are much higher. I lose my abiding peace. I notice my compassion toward others waning. I am cloaked in cynicism and insecurity. I have rebelled against You. I lose my childlike faith and instead sulk around in this place of teenage spiritual rebellion.

Thank You, God, my Heavenly Father, for showing mercy to me again and again. Thank You for Your forgiveness that evaporates my stubborn pride. Thank You for restoring my peace. Give me hope that someday I will come to You with my children and grandchildren and thank You for all that tough love and consistent parenting You showed me during the rebellious years. Help me, Father, to grow in my faithfulness to You.

Amen.

The ways of the LORD *are right; the righteous walk in them.*
HOSEA 14:9

Jehovah Tsidkenu, my Righteous Father,

The nations of the world are ruled by the works of men, but, Lord, You reign over all the earth. The laws of Your Spirit guide my life so that I can become as You. Open up Your ways to me so that I may study and live by Your statutes. No man can set a path for me that compares to Your loving ways. Lord, only You can lead me in the right direction, keep my feet always on the path, and help me find Your purpose for my life.

When I have prayed in times past for direction, You have answered in ways that comforted my fears and encouraged my heart. You are worthy to be praised for Your patience and loving commitment to Your children. Lord, because I am Your child, let Your will be done in my life. I will walk down the path that You have chosen for me. I will walk in the righteousness that came from the cross. I will follow Your Word and hide it in my heart. I will teach others to know You as I live for You each day.

Lord, I am determined to walk with You, following Your ways, all the days of my life!

Amen.

Everyone who calls on the name of L*ORD* *will be saved.*
JOEL 2:32

My Precious Savior,

Save me! Rescue me! Help me! Lord, today, like so many other days, I come running to You with another crisis to calm, problem to solve, and situation to fix. I need HELP. I am just one of six billion people on this planet, yet You hear and answer me when I call. How amazing to consider such love!

You love me so much that You willingly provide me with a means of escape. You are my only hope of rescue from a life filled with sin and despair. You put Yourself in the right place at the right time in order to save me from certain spiritual death. Lord, I've learned I can truly depend on You to bail me out in the big matters of life and death. You care enough to help me with those issues of eternal consequence. But I've also come to realize that You eagerly help me out in life's little crises as well. There is no problem too big or too small for You.

Today, as I come crying to You for help once again, I am filled with a comforting confidence that everything will be okay. I know that the God Who will never let me down will listen as I call.

Amen.

I will never forget anything they have done.
AMOS 8:7

God,

I know You won't forget the times we have been close—or the times I turned from You. Often, I have wandered away like the prodigal son. I found it appealing to live in a distant land far from You. Even with all You have given me, Lord, I have been foolish and arrogant. My headstrong independence often leads me in the wrong direction. I "live it up" for a while, only to find myself empty and starving for the peace that comes from fellowship with You.

There are periods of closeness and of distance in my human relationships. But unlike my human relationships, the separation is my failure, not Yours. You are always loving and merciful, and You wait for me to return. There have been times in my life when I've nurtured our relationship, made time to communicate with You, and spent time pondering Your truths. These are like times of homecoming. You are the gracious Father Who can see me when I am still far off and run to greet me. You embrace me and cry with joy. You insist on a party to celebrate my return.

Please keep me close to You, Lord. Don't let me forget the times when I have distanced myself, that I might remember how empty and meaningless life is apart from You. Thank You for remembering me.

Amen.

The kingdom will be the LORD's.
OBADIAH 21

Heavenly Father,

I watch the news and read the paper. Sometimes I wonder if it will ever be time for Your kingdom. So much pain. So much evil. Terrible tragedies happening to good people—some who seem to know You. There are days I can't wait until this whole heaven and earth are ruled by You and Your goodness.

What a day that will be. Evil will no longer reign. Every aspect of existence will acknowledge Your awesome love. The result will be astounding—a world ruled by love and peace rather than chaos and arrogant pride.

I believe that You are all-knowing. Help me to trust that You are reigning in my life, even when the grief seems to wash over me like a wave. Remind me that You are my King and by living in obedience to Your edicts, I will know calm in the storm. Give me chances to show Your love and power to those around me, so they can also know You as the King of love and mercy. Thank You for being such a tender and gracious ruler. If necessary, Lord, please prod, nudge, or drag me on the path of this life so that I can realize the plan You have for me and how I can have an impact upon the people in my life for Your kingdom.

Amen.

Those who cling to worthless idols forfeit the grace that could be theirs.
JONAH 2:8

God of Grace,

I have built so many false idols in my life I don't know where to begin. How much grace have I forfeited because, rather than coming to You with my needs, I go looking for fulfillment in money, possessions, friends, family, and even in church and religion? These things are worthless if I have no relationship with You.

The definition I have always heard for grace is: "God's unmerited favor." Please don't allow me to be foolish enough to forfeit something so valuable. Lord, send me a wake-up call the way You did when You sent Jonah to Nineveh. Remind me that You are not pleased when I put other things ahead of my relationship with You. Keep me mindful that in turning to these idols, I am not in a place to notice Your hand, held out and waiting.

Please, Lord God, forgive me for worshipping possessions, "churchiness," and even people, when I know You are the only One Who deserves this reverence. I am so grateful and full of praise for all You have brought me through so far. Build my faith in You so that my faith in these false gods will be diminished and even replaced with an abiding peace that only comes from living daily in the presence of the Almighty God.

Amen.

Rejoice not against me, O mine enemy: when I fall,
I shall arise;
when I sit in darkness, the LORD shall be
a light unto me.
MICAH 7:8 KJV

Lord,

Sometimes I think that the darkness is a good place to hide—a place to escape the reality of my defeat, lick my wounds, and consider my strategy. Even though human impulses drive me to the dark corners, You always meet me there.

Sometimes the darkness is not around me but within me. I get confused in the heat of the battle, fighting wars against spirits and powers of darkness. When the enemy wins a small victory, it sometimes appears to me like a big triumph—like I have fallen down, in my effort to follow You.

However, in the midst of my darkness—whether seeking solace or trying to understand the confusion—You bring light. You remind me that the battle is Yours, and the victory will be Yours as well. It is You Who turns my enemies away and promises that, though I fall, You will pick me up. Though the darkness surrounds me, You will shine the light of Your truth. And someday, all the battles will be won and darkness will disappear in the glorious light of Your eternal reign. Thank You for being my strength and my light in the dark times of life.

Amen.

The LORD is good, a refuge in times of trouble.
He cares for those who trust in him.
NAHUM 1:7

Lord,

You are so good! You have all power, and yet You stoop to care for me. You are a tower, a stronghold to which I can run in the day of trouble. How many times I have run to You, and You've always welcomed, comforted, and protected me. You know me, Lord, with all my faults and shortcomings, and yet You offer Your help and peace.

Help me never trust in my own strength, for it is foolish pride that makes me think I can handle things. Help me never to trust in people. Their strength too is faulty. I will fail, but You will never fail. Teach me never to place my trust in my circumstances. They will change. You never change. You are the perfect Father in Whom I can put my complete trust. You have my interests at heart. Your motives are pure and holy, rooted in love. Even though I was sinful You gave Your life for me. What earthly king or ruler would have done such a noble deed!

I safely rest in Your hands, Father, and have nothing to fear. Thank You for the peace and tranquillity I find in life, knowing that You are there for me. How good You are!

Amen.

The Sovereign LORD is my strength; he makes my feet like the feet of a deer,
he enables me to go on the heights.
HABAKKUK 3:19

Oh Lord,

The worries and cares of this world weigh me down like quicksand. Bills to pay, deadlines to meet, kids to carpool, groceries to buy, yard to mow, house to clean, running here, running there, fretting over a million different details of life in this physical world. It is so easy to get lost in the valley of the mundane, bogged down in the murky waters of discontent. As I energize my spirit through Your Word, give me the courage to climb up to a higher ground of spiritual maturity.

I pray that the physical side of living will not smother my spiritual life. When I get caught up in the cares of this world, remind me, Lord, that my soul will soar as I draw strength and vitality from You. Remind me that my life consists of more than "surface living." I can reach heights unknown by those who have not yet entered into a relationship with the Creator. Only as I am born again—born not just into physical life but spiritual life—can I know these higher dimensions.

Thank You, Lord, for the strength You provide. Today, please empower and enable me to climb above the here and now into Your majestic presence.

Amen.

Be silent before the Sovereign LORD, for the day of the LORD is near.
ZEPHANIAH 1:7

Dear Lord,

What do You have to say to me? When I spend time in silence and meditation, I realize that You want this from me so I can hear Your still, small voice. Sometimes it seems that with the silence comes a reverence I don't otherwise observe. Within the quiet, I find confidence in Your loving-kindness. My heart is peaceful as I stand in awe of You. Because I realize that You are in control of everything, it is easier to trust in Your care for me.

It is so difficult for me to strike that balance between trusting You and using this brain You have given me to make wise choices. Lord, You know that I want to be responsive and responsible, while still leaning on You with childlike faith.

Help me find more time to be with You and to be silent. I am a mother, daughter, wife, sister, and friend. These responsibilities keep me running at a pretty amazing pace. Please remind me that these "duties" are gifts from You. Bring me to a still and silent place where I can understand that this full life is a blessing from You. Show me mercy as I try to find more time to be silent and accept that all I have originates from You.

Amen.

From this day on I will bless you.
Haggai 2:19

Father God,

My heart is full with all of the ways You have blessed me. I cannot even count them. I am like the giddy child on Christmas morning who has so many gifts, she doesn't know which one to open first. You give and give. I am always receiving from You, blessing upon blessing.

It gives me great security to look into tomorrow and know You have already prepared more blessings. Too many times when I look into tomorrow, I see only question marks with exclamations of fear and worry. Instead, I need to look into the future with anticipation, expecting Your blessings.

From this day on, I will hear Your promise to bless. I will reject the urge to give any fear more power in my future than Your blessing. Even when death and pain do their worst, Your blessing redeems. Help me to understand that Your blessing is Your gracious kindness released into my life in such a free way that no reversal or circumstance can ensnare me. Help me realize that when I need anything more than I need You, I am in danger of missing Your blessing. From this day on, I will live a life more open to You. And from the depths of my blessed soul, I will live in gratitude.

Amen.

I will restore them because I have compassion on them. . . .
I am the LORD their God and I will answer them.
ZECHARIAH 10:6

Loving God,

Once again, I find myself wandering in a spiritual wilderness, feeling abandoned and lost. I'm not sure how I got here. I thought I was headed in the right direction but, somehow, I've veered off course. I realize now that I haven't been following You. Instead I've been running after the treasures that the world offers.

Each time, Lord, I find myself crying out to You, and in Your mercy You always answer me. What would I do if You chose not to respond? It fills me with dread just thinking about it. But by the wonder of Your love and grace, You created me in Your Own image. Therefore, You value me enough to attend to me, the one lost sheep, when I stray from the path.

It sometimes seems like a dream, to have been gifted with a love so vast and so deep that nothing, except my own narrowness, can keep it from me; I need only cry out and receive a blessing. But this is not an illusion; this is Your gift. If I believe in Your power to rescue me, I will never be lost. Loving God, I thank You.

Amen.

For you who revere my name,
the sun of righteousness will rise with healing in its wings.
MALACHI 4:2

Awesome God,

I know from the Scripture that fearing You is the first step to gaining wisdom. I used to think that "fear" meant to be in dread of You; but as I've become acquainted with You and Your nature, I've learned that it means to put You first in my life, to revere You as I would someone with great authority. You are worthy of my respect and adoration.

I know that You are the most important person in my life, and it is with great reverence that I worship such a majestic God as You, my Creator. I know that as I revere Your name and keep Your commandments, You will defend me and protect me from harm. You will keep me from the pitfalls that would otherwise entrap me.

Not only do You do this for me, dear God, but You also make the benefits of healing and the virtue of righteousness spring forth in my life. Surely life and health will radiate from Your throne and shine upon me, for You are mindful of me and do care for my needs. You bestow Your blessings upon Me as a caring parent to a trusting child, and I respond in awe and reverence to Your everlasting love.

Amen.

Seek first his kingdom and his righteousness,
and all these things will be given to you as well.
MATTHEW 6:33

Dear Lord,

It's so easy for me to get caught up in the desire for material things and the busyness of everyday living and forget to put You first in my life. But Father, I know how wrong that is. Teach me how to keep my life in balance, following the example You have set for me. Open my eyes and open my heart to true wealth, the kind that will last for eternity.

Help me always to keep my eyes on You, my first love. Teach me to seek Your kingdom and Your righteousness even before I contemplate my basic physical needs. Give me a spiritual hunger for You that overshadows even my hunger for food. Give me a thirst for Your heavenly water that makes my desire for earthly water pale in comparison. Clothe me in Your righteousness.

Oh Father, leave me with a vision of Your spiritual wealth. The rubies of compassion. The diamonds of contentment. The sapphires of charity. Never let me lose sight of the fact that You came to this earth and poured Yourself out for others as an example to me, that I too might pour myself out for others. Help me lose myself completely in You. Make my desires Yours. Make my thoughts Yours. Make me—all of me—Yours.

Amen.

Whatever you ask for in prayer,
believe that you have received it, and it will be yours.
MARK 11:24

My Blessed Creator,

How can I possibly thank You for all You do for me? Your blessings are endless! As I pray before Your throne with thanksgiving, I know Your mercies will never cease. Even before I pray, You know the needs of my heart. I know I can place my petitions before You because Christ has made a way for me to come to You directly, and You will always give the right answer to my requests. There is no prayer too small or too large for You.

Lord, You said, "Ask and you will receive" (John 16:24). We can claim this promise as ours! We can thank You in advance, knowing that Your perfect will is being done. Our Lord Jesus performed miracles too numerous to mention during His short time here. What peace it brings to know that miracles are still available to us today. Your Holy Spirit lives in our hearts, giving us the ability to accomplish what would be impossible on our own. Through You, Father, all things are possible. Hallelujah!

May I always receive Your answers with grateful worship, for You alone know the plans You have for my life. Let my spirit be humble before You, God—always giving thanks.

Amen.

The greatest among you should be like the youngest,
and the one who rules like the one who serves.
LUKE 22:26

Lord of the Universe,

How strange that You, the Creator and King of the cosmos, would choose to become a lowly peasant in a small country. Even more strange is the fact that You did so in order to accomplish the greatest feat in history: reconciling Your rebellious children (all of us) to Yourself and initiating an intimate, loving relationship with each of us. Because we are headstrong and stubborn and selfish, we fought You every step of the way. Yet You persisted and pursued us, not to coerce us but to convince us through the power of Your love.

Thank You, Father, for perfectly expressing Your love for me in Jesus. His willingness to serve, even to the point of death on the cross, demonstrated the depth of Your love. Give me the power and grace to follow His example. Make me a servant worthy of honor in Your upside-down kingdom. Help me identify with the poor and the powerless, with the sick and the aged. Give me a greater degree of empathy for their situations

As I share my resources with others, I will trust You to provide for my needs. Teach me to serve You and others with humility and joy.

Amen.

I have told you these things, so that in me you may have peace.
In this world you will have trouble.
But take heart! I have overcome the world.
JOHN 16:33

My Savior,

Like a solitary soldier struggling to get across enemy territory, I sometimes wonder if I'm ever really going to make it safely home. Maybe the battles I've fought have taken too much out of me. Maybe the losses I've suffered have robbed me of my resilience. Maybe I just don't have what it takes to finish the fight.

Thank You, Lord, for knowing my doubts. Thank You for seeing my struggles and reminding me that You are with me. Thank You for reassuring me that the victory has already been won. Being reminded that You have blazed a trail ahead of me does soothe my aching muscles. It helps so much to know I'm not waging a one-man war.

Father, please help me hold fast to the promises You have made to Your children. No matter how difficult things may get, never let me lose sight of the victorious future You have guaranteed for me. And as I march into combat each day, let me proudly display Your banner so the whole world will know that my heart has already been claimed in Your name.

Amen.

It is more blessed to give than to receive.
ACTS 20:35

Dear Giving Father,

You are the most generous of all givers. You have given us the prophets, Your Son, and a glimpse of eternity. You have given us all of Your creation, all of Your life, and all of Yourself. You give forgiveness, new life, and second chances. You give each new day, each new breath, and each new reason for faith. There is nothing to which You say, "This is too much to give."

Your gifts and blessings are rich and bountiful, Lord. So why do I find it so difficult to follow Your example? Why do I hesitate to bless others as You have blessed me? Am I a miser, stockpiling blessings, afraid I will lose my meager pile?

Oh, free me from such stinginess. I want the blessing attached to the gift, and so I make my list, long and wishful. Help me learn how backward that is, that the blessing is in the giving. Show me how to be a generous giver to those within an easy arm's reach, as well as those who require steps outside of my comfort zone. Teach me the mathematics of Your giving. May I give with joyful abandon, ignoring the cost in order to please You.

Amen.

Do not conform any longer to the pattern of this world,
but be transformed
by the renewing of your mind. Then you will be able
to test and approve
what God's will is—his good, pleasing and perfect will.
ROMANS 12:2

Wise Father,

I thank You for the gift of the Holy Spirit Who helps me discern Your will. You are the chief architect of my life. Lord, I am fearfully and wonderfully made by Your hands. And now that You have given me Your Son, I am equipped by Your great love to walk as You have designed.

Let my heart reveal the goodness of Your love. Let my mind meditate and express the power of Your redeeming covenant for mankind. Make me an offering that I may be a sweet scent before Your throne. There is nothing in this world that can satisfy like You.

As I think about You, Lord, my countenance fills with joy. Your goodness and mercy are as light radiating from a diamond and the sun sparkling on water. I no longer have to conform to this world, but I can rejoice in being molded and made into Your image. Your Holy Spirit teaches and guides. I want to be pleasing to You and know Your perfect will. Wise Father, my mind is renewed in You!

Amen.

Be on your guard; stand firm in the faith;
be men of courage; be strong.
1 CORINTHIANS 16:13

Dear Heavenly Father,

I want to be a person who never gives up, even when things seem unbearable. You have promised to never allow my load of responsibilities and problems to be more than I can bear. Knowing this gives me courage to face adverse circumstances and faith to know You will be with me, helping me.

Sometimes I do not have sufficient strength and self-will to go on, but I know You understand disappointment and heartache. You know how it feels to be misunderstood, and You give me strength when I feel I can no longer stand on my own. Help me never to lay down my Christian banner. When I feel alone and frightened, cause me to remember You will never leave nor forsake me.

May the vision of what I can be—through Your help—be stronger than the vision of who I am when overwhelmed by obstacles. Please give me the wisdom to realize that winning is not the only true victory. Dear Lord, You suffered the most degrading death, yet You won—in death was great victory. Help me die to my own self-will. May Your Holy Spirit bring a new birth of stability, faith, and courage.

Amen.

My grace is sufficient for you, for my power is made perfect in weakness.
2 CORINTHIANS 12:9

Heavenly Father,

Sometimes I start thinking I am strong and can handle everything life has to dish out by myself, especially after I've come through a tragedy or trial. In reality, I am nothing but a stumbling weakling without You. You and You alone are the reason I can survive.

Never let me forget the times I have trudged straight through one of life's tornadoes, head-bent into the ripping, black funnel, up to my hips in icy water and mud, only to have You walk to my side, put Your arms around me, and brace me as I choke against the flying debris. For Your grace is sufficient—perfect. Your power and strength reveal themselves in awesome sufficiency.

So when others ask, Lord, and shake their heads in admiring wonder, help me to remember to point to You, the One Who enables me to persevere, despite the storms of life. Engrave on my soul the picture of me and that funnel cloud and You, Lord—bigger than me and that tornado-like problem. While I cling to You for my very life, You enable me to stand firm. Gripping me tightly, You calm my trembling soul with Your strength. I need You, Lord, every minute of every day.

Amen.

The fruit of the Spirit is love, joy, peace, patience, kindness, goodness, faithfulness, gentleness and self-control. Against such things there is no law.
GALATIANS 5:22,23

Loving Father,

How easily I give in to my selfish nature! I don't always react in the way that I know I should, and at times I am frustrated by my weaknesses. I could make excuses and say that's just the way I am, but I know better. You promise that I am a new creation in You—the challenge is in the becoming.

Holy Spirit, I ask You to work in my heart and adjust my attitudes so my countenance radiates joy and peace. In difficult situations with others, may my responses be controlled with words that are carefully chosen and spoken in love—not anger. When I encounter people with imperfections not unlike my own, help me extend kindness and gentleness toward them—not condemnation or criticism. Help me rest in You and extend the same understanding to others that You have shown me.

Lord, thank You for the Holy Spirit Who is always present, comforting, and teaching me. Thank You for loving me in spite of myself. As I continue to walk daily with You, I pray that Your character will become more evident in my life. To know You is to be more like You. Today, may I produce much fruit for You.

Amen.

Be kind and compassionate to one another,
forgiving each other,
just as in Christ God forgave you.
EPHESIANS 4:32

My Loving Father,

Love is the basis for all Your actions toward Your children. You proved that by loving us and reaching out to us even before we were aware of You. You proved that by choosing us long before we even knew about You. You prove that still by extending forgiveness without question each time we ask.

And loving You, Lord, is pretty easy. That's because it's usually easy to return love when someone else loves us first. But to be the first to extend love—to take that chance—that is another matter altogether. I pray that You would make me willing to risk rejection by loving others as You have loved me. I will begin by setting my heart to readily and freely forgive those who wrong me. Would I be proving my love for You if I didn't forgive my brother when he offends me? You have forgiven me of a lifetime of offenses. And how could I refuse to extend help and kindness to those who need it when You have poured out Your mercy on me so many times?

Father, my sacrifices of kindness, compassion, and forgiveness are small things compared to the love You show me daily. Love is a wondrous thing! You are Love; teach me to love like You.

Amen.

Whatever is true, whatever is noble, whatever is right, whatever is pure, whatever is lovely, whatever is admirable—if anything is excellent or praiseworthy—think about such things.

PHILIPPIANS 4:8

Holy Lord,

I am overwhelmed with thoughts of what awaits me today. A battle rages within me as various people, situations, and challenges vie for my attention. My mind is an undisciplined and willful entity, not easily controlled. It is so easy to dwell on negative and self-defeating thoughts, to believe the worst. But Your desire is that my mind be centered on You and on Your truth.

And You, dear God, are all that is perfect. You are holy, just, and righteous. Every good and perfect thing has come from You. I see the beauty You have created everywhere—in crisp autumn days and glorious sunrises, in the faces of joyful little children, in the ethereal notes of a time-worn symphony—Your hand is evident.

In a world also filled with hatred, pain, and suffering, it is easy to believe that all is lost. But each day You show me a reason to hope, a glimpse of Your character in those whose lives are an example of that which is good and true. I choose to meditate on Your excellent gifts today. When I meet a challenge, show me at least one thing for which I can praise You. May my every thought be pleasing to You.

Amen.

Let your conversation be always full of grace,
seasoned with salt,
so that you may know how to answer everyone.
COLOSSIANS 4:6

Dear Father,

How can our conversation be always full of grace? We are human! Our lips are unclean, our tongues unruly, our words so often clamoring for attention or man's good opinion. And I am the worst offender!

Forgive me, Lord, for being so dense, so slow to listen, allowing my tongue to wag before my thoughts and words have been properly seasoned by You. I need Your Holy Spirit to prepare me to speak. I want the words that come from my lips to be honoring to You, filled with Your wisdom and goodness. Take my vain prattle, as good-intentioned as it may be, and transform it by the power of Your words; let my speech be so full of Your grace, Your compassion, Your selflessness that there will be no more room for my own foolish opinions and faulty judgments. Teach me to weigh my answers, producing them out of a clean heart, abundant with Your praise, with thanksgiving and wisdom.

Holy Spirit, season me. Flavor me with Your divine saltiness so that the words of my mouth and those things my heart mediates upon will be pleasing to You, Lord, my Rock and my Redeemer.

Amen.

Rejoice evermore. Pray without ceasing.
In every thing give thanks:
for this is the will of God in Christ Jesus concerning you.
1 THESSALONIANS 5:16-18 KJV

Heavenly Father,

I am so glad that I have found the source of true happiness. Now I don't have to hunt for it; I know exactly where to go when I have lost my joy. I know that You look after me at all times, and my joy comes from You. And as I come to You in prayer, You provide everything that I need. Thank You for this joy because it is a joy that the world cannot take away.

I thank You always because I know that something good comes out of every situation when You are allowed to control our lives. I pray that I will continually keep a submissive attitude toward You, that You may have control of my life at all times. I pray that the joy You give will be seen continually in my life and cause others to be blessed by the happiness that radiates from me. May I be a vessel that carries Your joy to others.

Thank You, Lord, for causing me to see the great benefit of praying continually, for this brings about the joy which is so important to the Christian life. I'm growing, Lord. And I'm learning. Help me learn something new about You every day.

Amen.

Now may the LORD *of peace himself give you peace at all times and in every way.*
2 THESSALONIANS 3:16

God,

I don't feel at peace today. Even when I'm rocking my baby girl before placing her in her crib, I feel restless. My thoughts are on the tasks that lie ahead. The peace You speak of seems impossible for me to embrace most of the time, much less at all times and in every way. When I look back on times I have known Your peace, they all have two things in common. My heart has been quiet, and there has been some reminder of Your awesome creative power.

I remember the time our family drove through a mountain pass without conversing. Looking out at the incredible beauty of Your creation, I felt Your peace in the wonder of Your creation. And I know that when I sneak to the bedside where a sweet, tiny head lies sleeping, and I reach out and touch my child's soft, innocent little hand, I am overwhelmed by peace in the presence of such a great gift—the gift of life.

God, please help me find a peace that goes beyond these moments. In the middle of the hectic morning rush, please remind my heart of that quiet place where You handle all the details. Don't let me fool myself into thinking that I have everything under control. Humble me and remind me that even I can experience Your peace at all times and in every way.

Amen.

Fight the good fight of the faith.
Take hold of the eternal life to which you were called.
1 TIMOTHY 6:12

Lord,

I want to thank You for the way You lead me into battle. Thank you also for Your love that will never let me fail. Lord, the good fight of faith keeps me holding onto You and standing on Your grace. Give me wisdom, and tell me of Your wondrous works. Equip me with the right weapons.

Lord, no army consists of one person, so teach me to fight together with my brothers and sisters. I am thankful for the strength they give me as we fight side by side. No matter how I stand or fall, I take hold of the promise in Your Word. It is a promise of good, and it has encouraged me. It is Your promise, that I will never have to fight without Your presence going before me. It is Your promise to sustain and strengthen me as I struggle for victory. It is Your promise never to leave my side until the battle is won. It is Your promise that nothing will be able to prevail against me; not sickness, trials, or temptation.

The promises of Your Word are true, and Heaven is my great reward. Lord, honor and glory belong to You forever!

Amen.

All Scripture is God-breathed and is useful for teaching, rebuking, correcting and training in righteousness, so that the man of God may be thoroughly equipped for every good work.
2 TIMOTHY 3:16,17

Exalted King,

You spoke in the beginning of time, and all things were created. You spoke to Abraham, and the promises of generations to come sprang forth from Your faithfulness. Lord, when I heard what Your Son had done for me, those words brought me life, and now I live in You. As I meditate on Your Word, I can see the awesomeness of Your power. Instruct me to know You even more through the revelation of Your Word.

As I set my heart to follow Your teaching, my life is changed for the better. Your words are a reflection of my situation and a recipe for hope. When there is no one to comfort me, Your words embrace me. When the storms around me begin to rage, I pray Your Word, believe Your Word, and call upon You. As Your words lead me, I am saved.

Help me to hold Your Word in my heart and live it in my life. I am equipped to know You, to serve You, to worship You, and to glorify You by Your Word. Let Your Spirit fill me with understanding and wisdom. Write Your Word on my heart, and breathe Your Word into my soul, exalted King!

Amen.

Remind the people to be subject to rulers and authorities,
to be obedient,
to be ready to do whatever is good.
TITUS 3:1

My Lord,

You have asked me to obey You; and because You are perfect and I respect and worship You, that's easy really. When I look at the world around me though, suddenly the picture changes. It often seems impossible to respect my earthly leaders. Even those who try to do good are flawed in so many ways.

The majority of our government leaders have engaged in shameful behavior. Many church leaders have done the same. Even my own father was not a man I could respect. So what am I to do, Lord? First of all, I know that I must remember to pray for our leaders fervently. As I lift them into Your care, I pray that You would convict them of any sins and renew their spirits. Let hearts be made right and let their decisions be based on Your Word, not the words of men. Keep their hearts free from greed, conceit, and malice, Lord; and let their actions be in Your perfect will.

Give me the patience to pray for these flawed leaders every day. Help me to give thanks for them, Father, and allow me to serve them in such a way as to please You. Thank You, Father, that through prayer, I can be obedient to You.

Amen.

The grace of the L*ORD* *Jesus Christ be with your spirit.*
PHILEMON 25

Dear Lord,

Unless I consciously pause during my day to recognize it, I sometimes overlook the grace You so graciously bestow on me each day. It is one of the greatest gifts I could receive, yet I find myself taking it for granted.

Nevertheless, You never withdraw Your gift from me. Your grace is with me the moment I awake, shining upon me like the warm morning rays. It clings to me on my way to work and overshadows me as I make my way through a busy day. And when I return home, I find Your grace gently resting on the wings of a setting sun, safely guiding me to my loved ones.

Despite this generous offering of grace, dear Lord, I sometimes find myself facing times of greater challenge, times when I need an additional measure of grace from You. When I face a task that is too difficult for me to handle, a problem too profound to judge, or when I've simply reached my end and don't know what else to do—that's when I need a special touch from You. During times like this, I pray for additional grace to get me through. Lord, please grace my spirit for such a time as this.

Amen.

Without faith it is impossible to please God,
because anyone who comes to him must believe that he exists
and that he rewards those who earnestly seek him.
HEBREWS 11:6

Sovereign God,

If faith pleases You, why do I stretch myself in so many other useless ways? Why do I struggle to make myself acceptable to You when I am only trying to please myself? All You want is faith, and too many times all I give are excuses for my lack of it.

Faith must start with an unfettered belief that You are the answer to every question. To place my trust in a circumstance, relationship, or possession is to exchange faith for sight. Help me recognize that seeing is not the same as believing—nor is understanding. Faith is not wishful thinking or some practiced positive attitude. Faith grows from the simple fact that You are everything You say You are. Grow in me a strong and fervent faith. Grow in me a faith that pleases You.

Thank You for every step of faith I take, no matter how small. Thank You for rewarding my efforts with more of Yourself. Take my "earnest attempts" at living out my faith, and deepen them, mature them, strip them of all impediments. Encourage me on this journey so that I may please You.

Amen.

Confess your sins to each other and pray for each other so that you may be healed.
The prayer of a righteous man is powerful and effective.
JAMES 5:16

Dear Listening Father,

In this world, You have surrounded me with a sea of others who know You. They are my fellowship and my accountability. They are in my thoughts, and their presence echoes in my prayers. Alone I am nothing more than a grain of sand, but together we are a beach, a coast, or even the world.

There are those whose existence seems merely a playground for jealousies and strife. Every word uttered from their lips is an arrow aimed at the heart of the unity of our fellowship. Hold us together, Lord. Let there be no missing member in the anatomy of this family. Together we can hold back the floods, and we can rescue the victims from the abuse this world strives to inflict upon them.

Hear my prayers, dear Father, and receive them with Your tender mercy. Help us to take Your message to those who do not understand the expanse of Your love. And make us an example of the kingdom we represent so others can understand why we choose to lay aside those things seen to follow after that which is unseen.

Amen.

Cast all your anxiety on him because he cares for you.
1 PETER 5:7

Loving Father,

You are so faithful and unchanging, an endless source of peace and assurance that surpasses my human understanding. You have demonstrated Your love for me in countless ways. Why then do I still doubt that You truly care for me? And even though I know You stand ready and waiting to take my burdens, why do I hold on to them so tightly?

You want me to freely give You everything that troubles me. Surely this is because You desire only the best for me and know the harm that worry causes. Unfortunately, letting go of my anxiety is not a simple thing for me. It is easier to believe I am able to manage my life if I fret over circumstances that are completely beyond my control. Why is that? Perhaps I am simply afraid to really trust You and to experience the perfect freedom that comes by allowing You to reign over my life.

Lord, today I lay all of my cares at Your feet, and I ask for joy and peace in their place. I know You are more than able to handle anything that concerns me, and I trust that Your wisdom is perfect. And in return, I promise to rest securely, knowing that You will never fail me. I am safe in Your hands.

Amen.

Make every effort to be found spotless, blameless and at peace with [God].
2 PETER 3:14

Holy God,

As I watch and await the fulfillment of Bible prophecy and the promise of the new heaven and earth, I fear that I might get so caught up with "doing" that I forget what a privilege "being" is. Because I live a fast-paced, active lifestyle, I am diligent not to forget that who I am is far more important than what I do. What kind of person am I on the inside, and what kind of person am I becoming?

Father, I want always to be found living as sinless a life as possible, doing Your will with no regrets. Living a spotless and blameless life, I've found, can only be accomplished by relying on the power of Your precious Holy Spirit. In my own strength, I could never be found perfect. I am forever thankful, Father, that when You command me to do something, You never leave me to accomplish the task alone. You always provide the Helper Who offers wisdom, power, and strength when needed.

Teach me to be serene and confident, free from fears, agitating passions, and moral conflicts—I want to be at peace. Show me, Lord, how to live in peace with others and with You. Father, when I am at peace, You are glorified.

Amen.

This is the confidence we have in approaching God: that if we ask anything according to his will, he hears us.
1 JOHN 5:14

My Loving, Affectionate Father,

So many times when I was a child, I looked up at my dad with questions and thoughts that puzzled my young mind. I would look up into my dad's eyes with eyes of innocence and wonder at the strength and assurance I found there. And although my thoughts may have seemed extraordinarily simple to him, he answered me with patience and understanding. I learned it was acceptable to ask ordinary questions—he would listen and he would love me.

As I matured I found that, much like my questions, life often poses some puzzling problems, and sometimes the answers can be just as complicated as the questions. I have found, Father God, that I can always ask You my toughest questions, and You always listen. Thank You for Your patience and understanding.

The psalmist says that You know all about me. Therefore, Father, I will continue to come to You with my questions, knowing that You surely hear me. I want You to know that no matter how old I grow or how puzzling the questions become, I'm still that wide-eyed child, and You'll forever be my loving, affectionate Father.

Amen.

Watch out that you do not lose what you have worked for, but that you may be rewarded fully.
2 JOHN 8

Lord,

Thank You for the promise of Heaven. There is nothing on earth that can compare with the rewards in Heaven. As I walk this life with You, I am encouraged that You have never left my side. When I have awakened in the middle of the night, You have always been there. During the day as I've faced the trials of this life, You have been with me. Lord, as the sun sets and the world slows down to rest, You are there. I am holding on to You.

My heart's cry is to run the race with You and fulfill Your will in my life. It is my desire to bring joy to Your heart and peace to mine. I am holding on to You. There is no greater pleasure I have than worshipping, proclaiming, and glorifying Your name. There is no greater joy than living according to Your plan for my life. I am holding on to You.

I desire to see Heaven, Lord, to sit at Your feet and cast crowns before You. I will keep my eyes on You until that day comes. There is still so much work to be done, and I am willing. Sweet, sweet Savior, strengthen me to keep holding on to You!

Amen.

Anyone who does what is good is from God.
Anyone who does what is evil has not seen God.
3 John 11

Oh God of All Goodness,

It is so easy to call "good" that which pleases me. It taints my definition with self-centeredness. Your definition of good does not include self-serving actions, even though goodness pleases You in and of itself. You define goodness with Your being. It encompasses Your whole identity. You are the essence of good, and only that which reveals Who You are is good. I cannot be good or do good with right actions, as loving and compassionate as they may be. My only hope for goodness is You guiding my action from the beginning, before I corrupt it with misguided motivation.

Have I tried to do good and in spite of all my trying disobeyed You so that my doing opened the door to evil? Protect me from such waywardness. It is not only the ignorant and rebellious who open the door to evil. When I try to do good without You, I am also an accomplice to evil.

Rescue me from false intentions. Fill me with Your impulse of love. Wrap me in Your discerning compassion. Counsel me with Your wisdom. Infuse my best effort with Your purity. Shape my attitudes and direct my actions so that whatever comes from me equals good because it came from You first.

Amen.

To the only God our Savior be glory, majesty, power and authority, through Jesus Christ our LORD, *before all ages, now and forevermore!*

JUDE 25

Most High God,

As I look, I can see Your glory and majesty displayed in the beauty of the world around me. From the softly babbling brooks to the crashing waves of the ocean, from the towering mountain peaks to the seemingly lifeless desert, Your glory and majesty are displayed everywhere. From the countless twinkling stars of the vast night sky to the mountains that smoke at the touch of Your finger, from the shaking of the earth to the tremendous winds that drive the ships at sea, Your power and authority are evident on the earth and in the heavens above.

All authority is Yours in Heaven and on earth. You accomplish Your will among the nations, placing leaders and removing leaders as You see fit. There is none like You—You are the only true God! Holy and blameless, just and merciful, You are the Bread of Life and the Light of the World. You have provided a way between humankind and the divine, between eternal life and death. You save us through Jesus Christ our Lord.

You are Savior and Lord from eternity to eternity. Splendor and majesty, all power and authority are Yours from the beginning. They are Yours forevermore! Glory and honor be to God!

Amen.

Here I am! I stand at the door and knock. If anyone hears my voice and opens the door,
I will come in and eat with him, and he with me.
REVELATIONS 3:20

Loving God,

You have knocked at the door of my heart and I have invited You to come in. What a wonderful mystery it is to know that the Creator of the universe lives inside me. I thank You, Lord, for coming to me when I could not come to You.

Now that You are a guest in my home, Father, I want more than anything for my life to be a home that is pleasing to You. I put away gossip, and lying, and thoughts that are not worthy of You. I will do my best to keep my home clean so that we can enjoy it together. I know there will be times, though, when I will fail to keep my promise. When that happens, I pray that You will be quick to speak, so I can know to ask for forgiveness and make things right.

Thank You, Lord, for placing Your faith in me, so much faith that You would come to live inside me. And thank You even more for Your promise never to leave me. You have honored me beyond measure.

Amen.

Additional copies of this book and other titles from Honor Books are available from your local bookstore.

If you have enjoyed this book and it has impacted your life, we would like to hear from you.
Please contact us at:

Honor Books
Department E
P.O. Box 55388
Tulsa, Oklahoma 74155
Or by e-mail at info@honorbooks.com

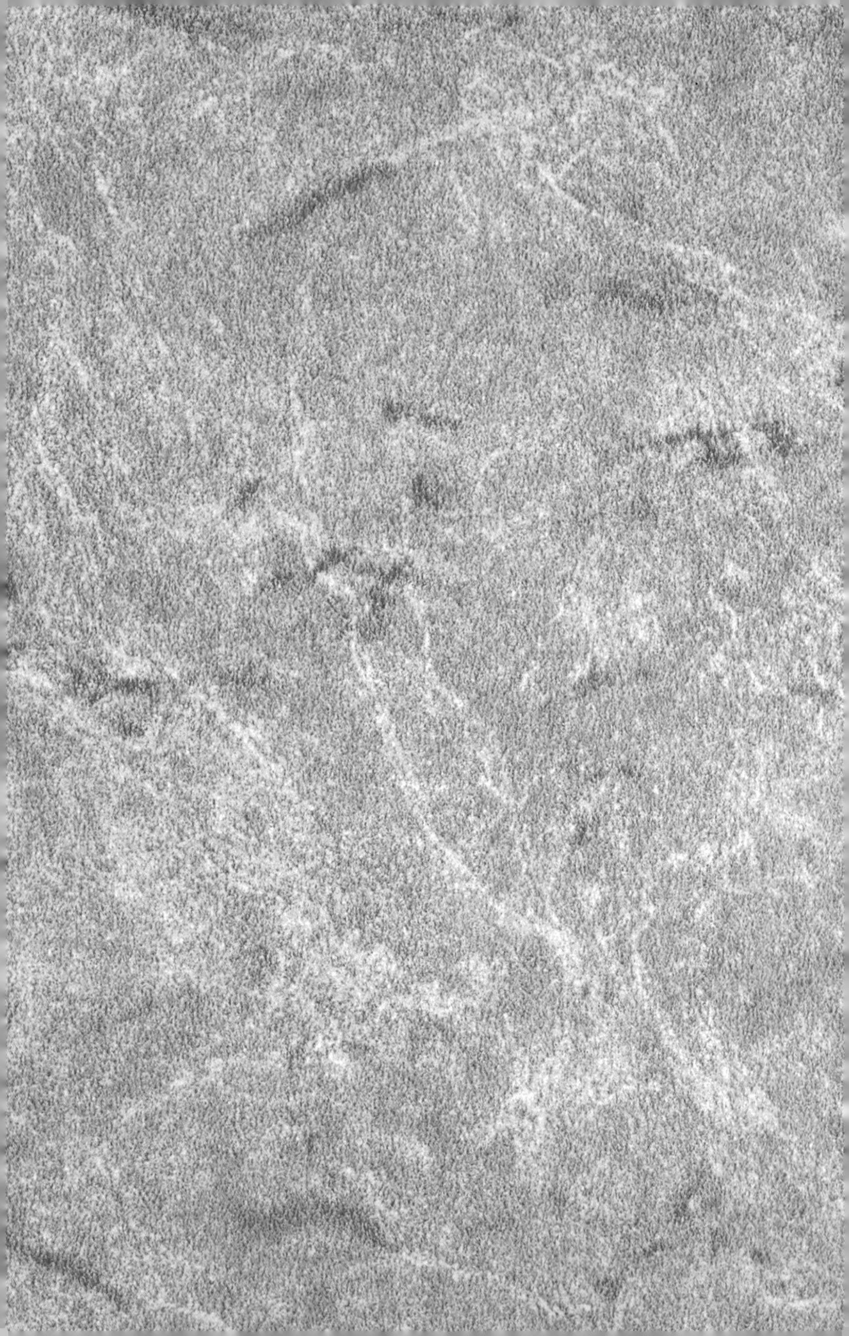